LOVE
LIKE JESUS

LOVE
LIKE JESUS

How Jesus Loved People
(and how you can love like Jesus)

KURT BENNETT

Love Like Jesus: How Jesus Loved People (and how you can love like Jesus)

First edition copyright © 2020
Second edition copyright © 2022

Unless otherwise noted, scripture references are from the English Standard Version of the Bible.

For information about this title or to order other books and/or electronic media, contact the publisher:

Enoch Media
Hillsboro, Oregon
kurt@kurtbennettbooks.com

ISBNs
Hardcover: 978-0-9841895-3-3
Softcover: 978-0-9841895-4-0
eBook 978-0-9841895-5-7

Second Edition

Printed in the United States of America

Cover and Interior design: 1106 Design

Contents

Part Two: Practical Help

Contents

Imitating Jesus

"I am the way," Jesus said.
JOHN 14:6

"Study Jesus," he said.

Only a few days after I retired from my job as a firefighter to start a career as a writer, I went to my pastor seeking guidance for this new phase of my life. I caught him in the parking lot after service and said, "Hey Jon, I just retired and I want to start writing about God, and eternity, and the things of the Lord. Do you have any advice for me?"

He looked at me intently, and said, "Study Jesus."

I was polite in my response—on the outside. But on the inside, I was doing an eye-roll. I thought to myself, "Study Jesus? I've been listening to you teach the Bible from cover to cover for years. Sunday mornings and Wednesday night Bible studies, for years. And after all those years, your advice for me is to study Jesus?"

But a few days later I reconsidered. "What do I have to lose?" I thought. And I decided to give it a try.

My life hasn't been the same since.

Before I made that intentional effort to study Jesus, my life was, I think, typical of most other Christians in America. Maybe it's typical of you. I went to church on Sunday. I worked. I tried to pray every morning (often squeezing it in during my drive to work). I ate. I slept. I went to youth soccer practices, school band concerts, and parent-teacher conferences. I tried to do the right thing. I tried to avoid doing the wrong thing.

That was life. I did my best. Sometimes I wondered if it would be enough for God. Usually, I rested in the redemptive work of Jesus on my behalf.

Then I began to study him.

In the course of doing so, I had that experience every Christian has had. Bible verses I had read many times before, suddenly had new and powerful meaning. One such verse was John 13:35 where Jesus says, "By this all people will know that you are my disciples, if you have love for one another." After reading those words of Jesus I had to ask myself,

"Is this what I'm known for? For my love for other disciples of Jesus?"

The answer was a resounding "No!"

I also came to realize much of the church in America has somehow glossed over certain passages in the Bible. Passages that instruct the follower of Christ to not merely confess Jesus as his or her Savior, but to imitate him.

John says of the Christ follower, "Whoever says he abides in him ought to walk in the same way in which he walked." When I read that I had to ask, "Am I really walking the way Jesus walked? I mean really?" (1 John 2:6)

Paul tells us directly, "Be imitators of me, as I am in Christ." This verse made me ask, "Am I imitating Paul and the people in my life who reflect Jesus' character?" (1 Corinthians 11:1)

Jesus himself said, "It is enough for the disciple to be like his teacher, and the servant like his master." This caused me to ask myself, "Who is my teacher? Who is my master? If it's Jesus, am I trying to be like my teacher?" (Matthew 10:25)

Jesus says in John 13:15, "For I have given you an example, that you also should do just as I have done to you." Speaking of this verse, Craig Keener in his classic IVP Bible Background Commentary says:

Disciples were to learn especially by imitating their teachers.[1]

Everybody's Imitating Somebody

Why isn't this idea of imitation emphasized more? It's profoundly important, yet it's not given the consideration it's due by the Western church. Curiously though, we see it in secular society. The great writers of today imitate the great writers before them. Great quarterbacks and point guards study the historical greats at their position. Facebook CEO Mark Zuckerberg studied Steve Jobs. Oprah Winfrey studied Maya Angelou.

When I was in high school, I read a book about the great basketball player Pete Maravich. He averaged 44 points per game in college: three years in a row. He was great in the NBA too. He's in the Basketball Hall of Fame. Some of the moves we see in the NBA today were pioneered by Maravich. He became one of my heroes, and I was inspired by his life. I was never much of a basketball player, but after I read about Maravich, I improved dramatically.

I read about how he was a gym rat, so I became a gym rat. I read about how he practiced, so I began to practice that way. I learned to shoot the way he shot. I learned some great basketball moves by imitating Pete Maravich's basketball moves. The result was that I played some of the best basketball of my life after imitating Maravich. Not that I ever approached his level. He was 6'5," I'm 5'11". He was fast,

I'm slow. He could jump, I can't. His dad was a D1 basketball coach, my dad wasn't. The list goes on. But even so, I improved dramatically after studying and imitating Pete Maravich to the best of my ability. (For another illustration of the power of imitation, check out "Kobe Bryant vs Michael Jordan—Identical Plays: The Last Dance (Part III)" on YouTube.)

Later, in a similar way, I imitated others to advance my career in the fire department. I found the best incident commander on our department, and I learned how to manage incidents the way he did. I found the best trainer on our department, and I trained the firefighters I was responsible for the way he did.

Something you should know about me is that I'm a bit of a nerd (some would say more than a bit). For a long time at the fire department, in addition to my normal duties, I was a one-man IT show, and I learned how to write code by imitating people who were much more talented than I was at writing code. Today my son Gabe is teaching me how to play a complicated Massively Multiplayer Online Role Playing-Game (MMORPG). *PC Gamer* says it's "the most difficult MMO you could ever attempt to play." I don't think I'd last a week in this game if it weren't for Gabe. My growth and enjoyment comes from imitating him. I imitate his tactics, his ship fits, and even his communication with other players. I'll never reach his level, but I can't imagine how overwhelming and stressful the process would be without Gabe to imitate.

So Much More

The book I read about Maravich was a thin, poorly written, cheaply made paperback of less than one hundred pages. At the time, there was no "Pete Maravich Master Class" on YouTube. None of my friends were big Maravich fans. I didn't have the help of Pete Maravich experts who could dissect how he played basketball. I didn't have much of anything. Just that crummy little book.

We have so much more in Jesus Christ. He left us his Gospels, the writings of his disciples, and the inspired Bible in its entirety. He left us with access to him through prayer. He left us with a community of people who also seek to conform to his likeness for us to connect with. He sent us His Holy Spirit. He's given us so much to help us imitate him.

Like my imitation of Maravich, or my imitation of Gabe, we'll never achieve the level of Jesus. Jesus is so much more than we are. But with the help of the Holy Spirit, when we're intentional about imitating Jesus, we can become so much more like him.

Imitating Jesus

To you and to me, Jesus says, "Take my yoke upon you, and learn from me, for I am gentle and lowly in heart, and you will find rest for your souls." Just take my yoke, Jesus says. He says, "I'll take one side, you take the other and walk in step with me. Imitate me." (Matthew 11:29)

We're given somewhere around 613 commandments in the Old Testament and 1,050 commandments in the New Testament. When I try to figure out how to follow them, it can be overwhelming and stressful. But when I imitate, it can just flow. I can find rest for my soul.

In the Western church today we tend to sit in pews and listen to lectures at the expense of imitation. That's where the emphasis lies for most Christians in most churches. I recognize there's value in listening to teachings. I'm a regular churchgoer, and I love listening to a great Bible teacher. My only point is that in the Western church today, lecture dominates.

In the Western church today, imitation of Jesus lives in the shadow of lecture, if it lives at all.

Yet Jesus commands us to imitate him. "A new commandment I give to you, that you love one another: just as I have loved you, you also are to love one another." (John 13:34)

". . . just as I have loved you."

Jesus is telling us: "Love just the way I loved."

Jesus is telling us to love like Jesus.

And that pastor told me, "Study Jesus." So I did. I went through the gospels from beginning to end, studying every interpersonal interaction of Jesus, studying everything he said and did, searching for any and every scrap of truth I could find about how Jesus loved people. My life hasn't been the same since.

What I learned about loving like Jesus is found in the pages of this book.

But before you continue, I should warn you: After studying these interactions of Jesus, I experienced profound and dramatic changes in my life. The same could happen for you.

Notes:
1. Craig S. Keener, *The IVP Bible Background Commentary: New Testament*, InterVarsity Press, 1993, p. 297

   Jason B. Hood, *Imitating God in Christ: Recapturing a Biblical Pattern*, IVP Academic, 2013 (cited as inspiration only)

Part One

Examples

CHAPTER 1

Love Like Jesus:

Billy Graham, Jim Bakker, and a Sinking Man

Jim Bakker and Kurt Bennett

I hated Jim Bakker. You know, the guy who was married to Tammy Faye. Jim was a televangelist to millions. Jim was a man who created a four-square-mile Christian theme park. Jim was also a man who sunk down to incredible lows. Jim Bakker was the man who admitted to having sex with his young secretary, and whose life hit bottom when he was convicted of fraud and sentenced to forty-five years in prison. From my perspective, Jim Bakker had a love for money more than a love of Christ. He lacked honesty and integrity. And he had a sex scandal thrown in for good measure. He was everything Jesus Christ is not. He misrepresented our Lord to millions.

Jim Bakker: I hated that guy.

Jim Bakker and Billy Graham

One day while Bakker was cleaning toilets in prison, a guard interrupted him. He thought he might be in some kind of trouble, but he soon found out he was pulled away from his toilet-cleaning duties because Billy Graham was there to visit him. Bakker walked into the room looking and smelling like, well, like a convict who was just interrupted from cleaning toilets. But Billy Graham held out his arms and embraced Jim Bakker. He told him he loved him. They talked. Then they prayed.

Later, a few days after Bakker was released from prison, Billy Graham's wife Ruth sat next to Bakker in church, pretty much declaring to the world, "Jim Bakker is my friend."[1, 2]

Jesus and Peter

Peter was in the same boat as the rest of the disciples when he saw a man walking toward him on top of the water. The disciples were terrified. But after discovering it was Jesus, Peter said, "Lord, if it's you, tell me to come to you on the water." And Jesus did just that. Then Peter began to walk toward Jesus, on the water, until his lack of faith got the better of him. Then he sank.

But Jesus reached down with his hand and pulled Peter up. (Matthew 14:25–33)

Peter lived with Jesus, knew the voice of Jesus, knew the smell of Jesus, and saw the miracles firsthand. But in spite of all that, after Jesus was arrested, Peter, upon hearing an accusation from a teenage girl, cursed and denied Jesus. But even though Peter sunk to the level of cursing and denying, even though Peter was at the center of this scandal, Jesus accepted Peter when he reinstated him after his resurrection. (Luke 22:56–62, John 21:15–17)

And beyond loving a person like Peter, Jesus loved people who struggled with sin and those living on the fringe of society. He loved prostitutes, lepers, and corrupt tax collectors. He loved people no one else wanted to love. People like Jim Bakker.

In the love chapter, 1 Corinthians 13, we're told that love always trusts. I've noticed in Jesus' relationships with his disciples, he always appeared to assume the best in others. He always seemed to give the benefit of the doubt. He always trusted. Peter could be a blunderer and a stumbler, yet Jesus seemed to trust him anyway. When the Pharisees asked Peter if he and his master paid the temple tax, Peter had no idea what the answer to that question was—but he answered anyway, incorrectly. Jesus responded to the situation with grace that amazes me. And after this incident, and after Peter's rebuke of Jesus, and after Peter called curses down upon himself and denied he even knew Jesus, Jesus continued to trust him, even giving him the responsibility to feed his sheep. (1 Corinthians 13:7 NIV, Matthew 17:24–27 and John 21:15–17)

Jesus and Judas

Even more amazing is how Jesus loved Judas. Even though Jesus knew all along that Judas would betray him:

After washing Judas's feet along with the rest of his disciples' feet, Jesus told them his betrayer was at the last supper: ". . . they began to question one another, which of them it could be who was going to do this."

One day I learned what this really means. It means Jesus' love for Judas was so genuine and complete that none of the disciples could tell which of them was Jesus' betrayer. When Judas left to betray Jesus, the other disciples thought he was on a grocery run.

5

Sometimes I wonder what Judas was thinking and feeling toward Jesus in those days and weeks before he did what he did. But regardless of what Judas was thinking and feeling, we see that Jesus loved him, even to the very end. (Luke 22:23, Matthew 26:50)

How to Love Like Jesus

When I learned how Billy Graham responded to Jim Bakker, I was confused and astonished. How could this be? How could Graham show such grace toward someone who repulsed people away from Christ? Away from the very person Graham spent his life trying to lead them to. It seems impossible to me.

But it also seems impossible to me that Jesus could stand on the water's surface, reach down, and pull Peter up. It seems impossible to me that Jesus would accept Peter the way he did, after Peter denied him, and even called curses down upon himself. It seems impossible to me that Jesus loved people on the margins the way he did. It seems impossible to me that Jesus loved Judas, his betrayer, the way he did. (Matthew 26:74)

Today some people see Jim Bakker as someone like Peter, a stumbler, bumbler, and fumbler whose life will be redeemed by God and used to bear fruit. Others see Jim Bakker as someone like Judas, a betrayer of Jesus whose life is irredeemable. But which side you or I may fall on isn't the point. The point is Jesus loves people in either category.

The people I know who love like Jesus don't let their feelings lead them to believe grace and mercy are impossible. They're likely to find a Jim Bakker-ish person, someone who's sunk to a new low, and though it seems impossible, by faith, stand on the water of grace and mercy, reach down, and pull them up.

That's what Billy and Ruth Graham did for Jim Bakker.

That's what Jesus did for Peter and people on the edge of society. That's how Jesus loved even Judas.

> *For God did not send his Son into the world to condemn the world, but in order that the world might be saved through him. (John 3:17)*

Notes:
1. David Aikman, *Billy Graham: His Life and Influence,* Thomas Nelson 2010
2. Jim Bakker, *I Was Wrong,* Thomas Nelson 1997

CHAPTER 2

Love Like Jesus:

Grace and Truth

*The woman answered him, "I have no husband." Jesus said
to her, "You are right in saying, 'I have no husband'; for you
have had five husbands, and the one you now have is not
your husband. What you have said is true."*
JOHN 4:17–18

How Jesus Loved People:
(Read John 4:7–45)

Jesus showed grace. In his conversation with the woman at the
well, he started by building a foundation of love. Throughout the
story, he continued laying this foundation by revealing himself to her
through conversation about the living water and the Messiah.

Then he shared truth. After, and only after, Jesus builds this foundation of love and grace, do we see Jesus begin to share truth. And
even then, we see him sandwich the first dose of truth between two
gracious statements. When she tells Jesus, "I have no husband," Jesus,
rather than railing on her for her past sins of promiscuity, says, "You

are right in saying you have no husband." He then shares his knowledge of her promiscuity, followed by, "What you have said is true."

He goes on to share with her the truth about Samaritan worship, and the kind of worshippers God seeks, those who worship in Spirit and truth. And he reveals the truth about his identity. Ultimately Jesus shows love to this woman by declaring himself to her. Speaking of Messiah, Jesus says,

"I who speak to you am he."

Confusing Pride with Principle

A twenty-something I know shared a conversation he had with a good lawyer. Right about now some of you are saying to yourselves, the word *good* and the word *lawyer* don't belong in the same sentence. But I know this man personally, and although good lawyers might be rare, this attorney is one of them. He's a skilled lawyer, and beyond that, he's a good person. He has a heart for the underdog, and he strives to do his best for every client. This lawyer made a statement to my friend that surprised me. He said,

"The best lawyers are not those who love to win an argument."

When I heard that, I thought to myself, "I know this can't be true—because I've seen all the lawyer TV shows: *The Good Wife*, *Better Call Saul*, *Boston Legal*, *Law and Order* . . . Those lawyers always win the argument. And they seem to relish the courtroom confrontation.

But the good lawyer says the best don't take pleasure in winning the debate. He says the best are outcome oriented. He says the best don't look for ways to win the argument, they look for ways to reach the best possible result. At the end of the discussion he made this statement:

"Never confuse pride with principle."

I had to think about that. How many times did I believe I was standing on principle, when in reality, what I was after was victory and conquest, so I could feed my pride? And this was nearly always at the expense of outcome, and very often at the expense of the relationship.

Contrast that with what we see in our story, which is how unmistakable Jesus' love is. It's unmistakable to the reader, and most importantly, it's unmistakable to the Samaritan woman at the well. And look at the result. She left that conversation to gather up and bring the townspeople to Jesus, and she did it because she knew Jesus loved her. Yes, the truth was shared, but only in the context of Jesus' unmistakable love.

The Lesbian College Professor Who Hated Christianity

Rosaria Butterfield was a college professor, and a lesbian, who hated Christianity. Actually, *hate* is too mild a word, she *reviled* Christianity. Here's how she felt about it, in her own words: "Stupid. Pointless. Menacing. That's what I thought of Christians and their god Jesus, who in paintings looked as powerful as a Breck Shampoo commercial model."

In 1997 she wrote an article for her local newspaper attacking the Christian group Promise Keepers. Perhaps not surprisingly, she received a great deal of mail as a result of that article. Many responses were from Christians who attacked her views, and many were also from people who applauded her position. But one response didn't fit into either category. A pastor sent a letter she described as kind and inquiring. She threw it out. Then later she fished it out of her recycle bin. She stared at it for a week before she decided to accept his invitation to dinner.

Dinner led to friendship with the pastor and his wife. Friendship led to her reading the Bible. Then she read multiple translations of the Bible. After two years, she came to the place where she was painfully conflicted. She believed. She believed in the gospels and what they said, and she believed in Christ. But she struggled mightily with the cost of conversion. Her circle of friends wouldn't receive the news well if she gave herself to Jesus. But she did anyway.

Today she's married to a pastor.[1]

So often my own tendency is to see what I think are flaws in people. Then I try to "help" by pointing out their flaws or wrong thinking, so they can be fixed, so the person can be made more perfect; and that's important, because, I reason, I love that person and I want to see them "improve."

I've traveled down that road thousands of times, and I've seen no fruit come from that tree. The truth is, it's not even a tree. It's a dead stick that I beat people over the head with. Sometimes it made me feel better, but the results just aren't found there. The pastor who led Rosaria Butterfield to Jesus didn't approach her that way. The good lawyer doesn't approach people that way. Jesus didn't approach people that way.

How to Love Like Jesus

So here's how you and I can love people like Jesus. When you're sharing truth, it's essential your love for the person you're talking with be unmistakable. Unmistakable to you, to any observers, and, most importantly, to the person you're sharing with. When you're sharing truth, the person you're talking with has to *know* you love them. When you're sharing truth, you have to do so with a heart filled with Christ's love.

Just as soon as your inner prosecuting attorney begins to rise up, the result you're looking for is destroyed.

Of course, Jesus was a master at sharing truth in love. In the gospels we see him share this way over and over.

But you and I have to recognize that while Jesus was a master at this, you and I may not be. (see John 1:20) For me, I *know* I am definitely not a master at sharing truth in love.

The people I know who love like Jesus keep all of this in mind, and when they're tempted to share truth with someone, and they begin to feel God's love leaving their heart, they choose not to share at all.

If they begin to feel God's love leaving their heart, they just keep their mouth closed.

If they begin to feel God's love leaving their heart, they walk away, or they change the subject to one where there's common ground.

Because if I choose to share without love, it's likely I'll only cause that person to become further entrenched in their current position.

But if I share in unmistakable love, I give the Holy Spirit the best possible chance to reach that person.

The people I know who love like Jesus build a foundation of grace and love, first. And share truth only when their love for the person they're sharing with is unmistakable.

That's how Jesus loved people.

> *If I speak in the tongues of men and of angels, but have not love, I am a noisy gong or a clanging cymbal.*
> *1 Corinthians 13:1*

Notes:
1. Rosaria Champagne Butterfield, *The Secret Thoughts of an Unlikely Convert: An English Professor's Journey into Christian Faith*, Crown & Covenant, 2012

CHAPTER 3

Love Like Jesus:

Jesus and the Critic

When Philip found Nathanael he said to him,
"We found the one Moses and the prophets wrote
about, Jesus of Nazareth, the son of Joseph."
Nathanael said, "Can anything good come out of Nazareth?"
Philip said, "Come and see."
As Nathanael approached Jesus, Jesus said, "Behold,
an Israelite indeed, in whom there is no deceit."
Nathanael said, "How do you know me?"
Jesus answered, "Before Philip called you,
I saw you under that fig tree."
Nathanael said, "Rabbi, you are the Son
of God. You are the King of Israel."
Jesus said, "Because I saw you under that fig tree you
believe? You'll see greater things than these."
JOHN 1:45–50

15

How Jesus Loved People:

Critical and cynical. That was Nathanael's attitude toward the news Philip had "found the one Moses and the prophets wrote about."

"Nazareth! Can anything good come from there?" Nathanael responded.

At the time, Nazareth didn't have the best reputation as a city. It may be Nathanael's cynicism and criticism were understandable. However, to Nathanael's credit, though he has some tough questions, he decides to accept Philip's invitation to "Come and see" for himself.

And here's how Jesus responds to Nathanael's negativity.

"Behold, an Israelite indeed, in whom there is no deceit," Jesus says enthusiastically as he sees Nathanael approaching.

"Behold, an Israelite . . ." The very first words out of Jesus' mouth are words affirming Nathanael as an Israelite, as one of God's chosen people.

". . . in whom there is no deceit!" (or guile as the King James Version renders it). This was a play on words by Jesus. He was referring back to Jacob. Jacob, who was renamed Israel by the Lord, was a man known for his guile and deceit. You probably remember Jacob tricking his blind father Isaac out of his older brother's blessing. One of a number of instances where Jacob used deceit and guile to get his way. So here we see Jesus, rather than defending Himself against Nathanael's cynicism, using this play on words to emphasize Nathanael's genuineness and honesty.

Nathanael, recognizing Jesus knew how he felt about a prophet coming from Nazareth, says, "How do you know me?"

"Before Philip called you, I saw you under that fig tree," Jesus replies.

At which point Nathanael answers, "Rabbi, You are the Son of God. You are the King of Israel."

And Jesus answers back, "Because I saw you under that fig tree you believe? You'll see greater things than these." Jesus finishes the conversation by commending Nathanael for his faith.

A Quarterback, a Fire Chief, and a Pastor Respond to Criticism
A friend who used to work security in a football stadium told me about this encounter he saw between a Chicago Bears' quarterback and a man who was destitute. The QB arrived at the field early before a game and was walking into the stadium when this guy who appeared to be homeless "accosted" him. He grabbed the QB's arm and started telling the quarterback how to do his job. He went on and on about how this quarterback could improve his play on the field. The quarterback remained silent during the whole episode. Much to my friend's amazement, when the man finally ran out of steam, the quarterback said, "I appreciate your suggestions, and I'll try to keep them in mind for the game. It was nice talking to you." (For more on this quarterback see the "Notes" section at the end of this chapter.)

I saw a new fire chief do something similar one time when one of our senior captains on the department laid into him for changing a policy. This senior captain was yelling obscenities and making crazy accusations, right in front of a group of firefighters. The new chief remained calm and didn't say much of anything in response.

Another time I saw a pastor get lambasted by an elder in a leadership meeting. This pastor just sat there on his stool, in front of the group of fifty or so elders, and he just, well, he just listened. During the entire diatribe, his expression was one of thoughtfulness. And after the "accuser" was through, the pastor simply responded with, "Huh." But the way he said it, he spoke in a tone that said, "OK, I hear what you're saying, and I will think about it." The "accuser" was satisfied, and the pastor then moved on to the next agenda item.

Navy Seals (and How to Stay Calm During a Firefight)
I'm not particularly good at responding to criticism the way the quarterback, fire chief, and pastor did in the examples above. I tend to get defensive. I can feel my blood pressure rising as the critic continues to castigate me.

But there are some breathing techniques Navy Seals use to stay calm during firefights. While running into burning buildings as a firefighter, I've found breathing techniques like the ones the Seals use to be very helpful. During firefights or other stressful combat situations, Seals simply inhale, filling their lungs belly first, diaphragm second, upper chest last, for a count of four. And then they exhale for a count of eight. Another technique Seals use is to fill their lungs in the same way for a count of four, hold their breath for a count of four, exhale for a count of four, hold their breath for a count of four, and then inhale for a count of four, and so on (this is called "box breathing").

These techniques haven't just helped me while plunging into a burning building, they've also helped me to respond more like Jesus to combative critics.[1]

Five Ways to Make Criticism Sting Less (and help us to grow from it)
Some of the best advice I've seen about responding like Jesus to criticism comes from a blog post by a podcaster and pastor named Carey Nieuwhof. According to Carey, there are five things you can do to make criticism sting less and help you grow more.[2]

1. *Don't respond for twenty-four hours.*
   If you're like me, when you receive criticism, you become flooded with emotion. You feel anger, or you feel deflated, or you feel crushed, or a combination of any number of emotions. I've learned over the years that nothing good happens

while I'm upset. If I try to address criticism while I'm upset, I make it worse instead of better, even when I think I'm saying or doing the best thing in the moment.

Most of us are the same. So just thank them for sharing or say nothing, or even walk away if you have to. And then wait a day. Let yourself sleep on it. Give yourself time to go to God and ask Him about it.

The people I see who respond like Jesus to criticism respond with grace and integrity. Waiting for twenty-four hours gives you the best possible chance to do the same. What a difference a day will make in your perspective, and in your quest to love like Jesus.

2. *Ask yourself: Is there any truth at all in what they said?*

Jesus is the one person in the history of the planet who never had to ask himself this question. But for the rest of us, it will be rare for us to examine what was said and come to the conclusion there was no truth in it. And if you do come to that conclusion, ask a friend who knows you well, someone you trust, if they see any truth in what was said. They might see what the critic saw, even if you don't.

And even if you find some small truth in there somewhere, use it to grow into a better person. Use it to grow into a person who's more like Jesus.

Finally, even if there's no truth whatsoever in what was said, at least you asked. You lose nothing by asking.

3. *Own what you can.*

Find whatever part of the criticism you can own, even if it's small. Try to understand how that person came to feel the way he or she does.

Try to understand the why behind their feelings, even if they overreacted.

I've noticed that people who are successfully loving like Jesus take responsibility. People who struggle to love like Jesus tend to blame.

4. *Raise the relational bar.*

Raise the level of communication from how they communicated with you.

If they emailed you, call them.

If they called you, take them out for coffee. Tell them you'd like to learn more about what they said and how they're feeling.

If they criticized you in person, take them out to lunch.

I've experienced this both as a critic, and as the one being criticized, and it's amazing how disarming it can be. If the person who criticized is healthy, and if you own whatever you can, most of the time the situation will be diffused and you'll experience a spirit of reconciliation—if you raise the relational bar in this way.

5. *Discard the rubbish.*

Even if you found some truth you could own, and you responded with grace and love, the way Jesus would have, sometimes there's still rubbish to be dealt with. And the way to deal with it is to discard it.

Oftentimes criticism is less about you and more about what's going on with the critic. Maybe they just had a fight with their spouse. Or maybe they just got dumped on at work. Or maybe they're depleted physically, or emotionally.

Sometimes good people overreact, or react inappropriately. And sometimes critics aren't just mad at you, they're mad at the world. Either way, it's likely there's some content in their criticism that's not based in reality. It's based in something else: something having to do with the critic more than the one criticized.

Share it with God. Talk to a trusted friend about it. Acknowledge that it hurts anyway. And then let it go. Don't carry a load from yesterday into today.

How to Love Like Jesus

Jesus could have responded to Nathanael with a whopping comeback.

"You obviously don't know Who (with a capital W) you're talking to, or what you're talking about. I wasn't even born in Nazareth, I was born in Bethlehem, the precise place where God promised the Messiah would come from. Maybe you should get your facts straight before you share your cynicism. I was going to include you in a group of eleven people who will turn the world upside down and influence the entire planet for eternity, but with that attitude—you're out!"

But that's not what Jesus did. Instead, he met Nathanael's negativity and cynicism with grace and love. Jesus, rather than defending Himself, responds to Nathanael's attitude by affirming Nathanael's position as one of God's chosen, by emphasizing his honesty, and by commending him for his faith.

Jesus took Nathanael's negative and turned it around to a positive, and he communicated with Nathanael in person.

It's so easy to respond to someone who's critical toward you with defensiveness, or by returning the negative with a negative shot right back. But the people I observe who love critics the way Jesus did, look for whatever positive they can find, there's always something, and they start there, and they often raise the relational bar too.

The people I know who add value to critics the way Jesus did, have more opportunity to impact their life for Christ. The people I know who take value away from critics, even when they're well-meaning, tend to cause others to withdraw from them and to disregard what they have to say.

So next time you're faced with a critic or a cynic, start by finding and emphasizing the positive. Raise the relational bar.

Jesus did.

You can too.

Notes:
- The quarterback for the Chicago Bears was Bill Wade. Wade was the QB for the Bears when they won the championship in 1963. My friend tells me that after the encounter, the destitute guy was beaming with pride. Today the Bears play at Soldier Field, but when this incident occurred they played at Wrigley.
- Before Tim Tebow, Bill Wade was an NFL quarterback who was into evangelism. He used to pass out a pamphlet he created called, "Quarterback for Christ." In that tract, Wade describes his relationship with Jesus.

Excerpt from Bill Wade's "Quarterback for Christ":

Bill Wade—Quarterback for Christ[3]

Therefore if any man be in Christ, he is a new creature: old things are passed away; behold, all things are become new.
—2 Corinthians 5:17

When sports writers and others ask me for my greatest thrill, they no doubt have in mind some dramatic game or specific play that occurred during my collegiate years at Vanderbilt University, my seven years with the Los Angeles Rams, or my experience with the Chicago Bears. They are usually surprised at my reply.

First of all, my most thrilling moment in football is yet to come. In the game of life, however, my most thrilling moment to date would have to be the decision I made after Navy officer Jim Wilson talked to me for about six hours back in 1953. Though I had been brought up in a Christian home, with wonderfully devout parents, Jim impressed upon me the necessity for a personal surrender to Jesus Christ as Saviour and Lord. A new aim and purpose in my life resulted from my spiritual transaction at that time.

In the game of pro football, there are many injuries which could be avoided. The best way to escape these is to keep your body physically fit.

When we consider life, whether it be for ten years or a hundred, we are participating in a series of games. We will readily admit that the game of life is basically spiritual. As we play the game and learn our purpose, whether it be president of a bank, worker in a factory, secretary, or quarterback of a football team, we must exercise ourselves spiritually to win the daily battles.

I have found there are three basic exercises which strengthen me spiritually. The first is the exercise of prayer. The second is that of reading the Bible. The third is one that is vital to every Christian—that of asking in prayer each day that you might be allowed to talk to someone about the Christian way of life.

If you believe that God has created you, it becomes a supplemental belief that He has created you for a purpose. What purpose? This is answered when we submit ourselves to Him, that His will be done in our lives.

In talking to youth groups on the subject of "What It Takes To Play Football," I like this acrostic:

C—Confidence ". . . If God be for us, who can be against us?" (Romans 8:31).

H—Humility. ". . . he that humbles himself shall be exalted" (Luke 14:11).

R—Respect. We must have a respect for laws, of doing what is right. A healthy respect for others is vital to a fruitful Christian life.

I—Intelligence. As a quarterback, one must learn and know a great many things. To be good, useful Christians, we should be as intelligent as possible.

S—Sincerity. You must be sincere before people will believe you.

T—Truth. "Unto thine own self be true." Don't lie to yourself. Don't try to fool yourself by fooling others.

We can belong to Christ by opening our hearts, allowing Him to cleanse us from our sin, and personally accepting Him as Saviour and Lord of our life.

Prayer Suggestion

Open up all the way to Jesus Christ. Let Him guide you into a wonderful new life.

1 Sealfit.com
2 Carey Nieuwhof, *5 Ways To Make Criticism Sting Less*, CareyNieuwhof.com
3 Larry Norris, *VanderBears: Jay Cutler Now and Bill Wade Then*, Sporting Chance Press Talk

CHAPTER 4

Love Like Jesus:

Jesus and the Control Freak

Hard Questions

Michael is thirty-four years old, married, with no kids. He's one of my closest friends, and he's also someone who's always asking these great questions about the Bible: provocative questions, hard questions, but great questions. And it's caused me to look at the Bible differently. I read and hear so much about how the Bible is restrictive. But this person with the questions has me thinking about the freedom God has given us. Freedom to make our own choices. Have you ever considered how God arranged things in the Garden of Eden? Adam and Eve had the thinnest Bible in history. There was only one rule: Don't eat from that one tree.

And have you ever considered what's not illegal in the Old Testament? Polygamy, for instance, was not illegal. And prostitution was decriminalized, if you will. I'm not saying either of those is good, I'm just saying neither of those was a felony in the civil code given to Israel in the Old Testament. People were free to engage in those activities without significant legal repercussions, though the spiritual ramifications and life consequences were still there (see Proverbs 23:27 and 29:3).

The point is, God is radical when it comes to our freedom. He wants us to have the freedom to do what we want, even when it's wrong. God's perspective seems to be that demanding someone do something, or guilting them, or coercing them, is not an act of love. That realization really made me look at my own ideas about what God wants *me* to do concerning the behavior of others. Because sometimes *I* want other people to do what *I* want them to do, and *I* can get frustrated when they don't.

Maybe you've been there. Maybe you *are* there. Maybe you want to spend money a certain way but your wife wants to do it her way. Or maybe you want to drive a certain way but someone in the car wants to go another way. Or maybe you want more time to recreate with the guys, but she has other ideas. Or maybe it's just you and your wife trying to decide what to do for dinner. Whatever it is, our perspective changes when we see the enormous respect Jesus demonstrated for the free will of others.

How Jesus Loved People: He Asked

"What do you want me to do for you?" Jesus asked the blind man sitting by the road near Jericho. (Luke 18:38–41)

"Do you want to be healed?" Jesus asked the invalid at the pool of Bethesda. (John 5:6)

"Shall I come to heal him?" Jesus asked the centurion with the paralyzed servant. (Matthew 8:7 NIV)

"Will you give me a drink?" Jesus asked the Samaritan woman at the well. (John 4:7 NIV)

26

He asked. He asked people what it was that they wanted, or even *if* they wanted. He left the choice up to them.

Jesus Let People Choose

The people of the Gerasenes were afraid of Jesus and they "asked him to depart from them." So Jesus got into a boat and left. (Luke 8:34–37)

When the people of Samaria asked Jesus to stay with them, he interrupted his itinerary and stayed with them for two days. (John 4:39–41)

Ever notice that Jesus never went out looking for individual Pharisees to engage? Nicodemus had to come to Jesus. (John 3:1–21)

And then there's the guy driving demons out in Jesus' name: "Master," said John, "we saw someone driving out demons in your name and we tried to stop him, because he is not one of us."

"Do not stop him," Jesus said. (Luke 9:50)

And there's the synagogue official who told the people not to come on the Sabbath to be healed. But Jesus said, No! Let them come! (Luke 13:14–17)

Even his own disciples tried to constrain the will of certain people. They refused to let the little children come to Jesus. And when Jesus saw this, he was indignant. No! He said, Let them come! (Mark 10:14)

Finally, there's Judas objecting to Mary pouring her perfume out onto Jesus' feet. How did Jesus respond? He said, Leave her alone! (John 12:3–7)

Even when it broke cultural convention, Jesus gave people the freedom to do what they wanted to do.

Even Hostile People Were Given the Freedom to Choose

When the prodigal son demanded his inheritance, his tone was more bitter and cold toward his father than most people realize. In that culture, at that time, when a son demanded his inheritance in that way, what he was saying to his father was, "I wish you were dead. Your being alive, your very existence, is getting in the way of my inheritance." But what does the father, who represents God in the parable, what does he do? Amazingly, he lets the prodigal do what he wishes. (Luke 15:11–32)

How to Love Like Jesus

There are exceptions, of course. With a stern countenance, Jesus imposed his will on the demons he cast out of people. (Luke 4:35) And when Peter cut off an ear with his sword, Jesus said, "No more of this!" (Luke 22:51) But, the general pattern we see from Jesus is to allow people to do as they wish. Even when Judas came to betray him, Jesus didn't try to talk him out of it. He simply said, "Friend, do what you came to do." (Matthew 26:50)

It's puzzling to me, the way Jesus is so enthralled with the idea of free will. I'm the kind of person who likes to arrange things so they can't miss. I would have put a fence around the forbidden tree in the garden. I would have taken Samson on a retreat until he cooled off on Delilah. I would have made sure Bathsheba's bathtub wasn't in view of David's palace.

But God doesn't do things that way. He set things up exactly the opposite. God always ensures choice. He arranged the universe so we have freedom. He's completely committed to this idea of free will.

So for me, and for you, to love like Jesus, we need to rethink our expectations of others. Love requires a choice. When we demand, coerce, or guilt someone into doing something, we don't love them the way Jesus loved.

Jesus demonstrated a radical respect for the freedom of others to choose to do what they want to do.

The people I observe loving like Jesus also show that same radical respect for people's freedom.

That's how Jesus loved people.

That's how you can love like Jesus.

After he finished a parable or a teaching Jesus would often say, "He who has ears to hear, let him hear." (Luke 8:8) In other words, Whoever hears hears, and whoever doesn't want to hear doesn't hear.

The choice is yours.

CHAPTER 5

Love Like Jesus

Touch

While he was in one of the cities, there came a man full of leprosy. And when he saw Jesus, he fell on his face and begged him, "Lord, if you will, you can make me clean." And Jesus stretched out his hand and touched him . . .

LUKE 5:12–13

How Jesus Loved People

The life of a leper was one of isolation. The law demanded he live alone. His clothes were to be rent, his head bare, and wherever he went he was to announce his defiled condition to those around him by shouting, "Unclean, unclean!" (Leviticus 13:45–46 KJV)

There was also a law against others touching a leper. Most people would find it revolting anyway. A leper had skin lesions and deformities.

But Jesus reached out his hand, and touched him.

How to Love Like Jesus

A friend who does counseling once told me a patient of his came back to visit him a few years after her counseling sessions had ended. She was doing extremely well and credited my counselor friend with her improvement.

"What was it that made the difference?" he asked. "The wisdom I shared? My insights into your family life perhaps?"

"No," she replied. "It was the hugs."

A few years ago I read a fascinating article about the power of physical touch. Patients touched by their doctor perceived their visits to have lasted twice as long as patients who weren't touched. Students who were touched by their teachers were twice as likely to volunteer in class. The human touch can ease depression. The human touch can improve relationships.

In a Cal Berkeley study, touches among NBA teammates were measured. Among all NBA teams, who do you suppose touched the most? The top two were the Boston Celtics and the L.A. Lakers—the two most recent NBA champions at the time of the study.[1]

I love living in the information age. I love Google, and Instagram, and Twitter, and YouTube. I feel blessed to live in an age when all this is available. But I also know I can have a tendency to become immersed in what I'm doing on my phone, to the exclusion of real-life face-to-face interaction with human beings.

It puts me at risk of neglect for showing people love through touch.

And touching, appropriately of course, is one of the most effective ways of communicating love to others.

Imagine with me what Jesus' touch must have meant to that leper from our story. Picture living in a society where it was illegal to touch a leper. Put yourself in the leper's shoes and think what it would be like to shout out, "Unclean, unclean," so people could stay clear of you, and completely avoid any possibility of touching you. It's hard to think of someone who would crave the touch of another human more.

Jesus didn't have to touch anyone. He once said to a centurion, "Go; let it be done for you as you have believed." And the servant, who was nowhere near Jesus physically, was healed at that very moment. Jesus, the Son of God, had the power to heal without touching. But he nearly always chose to touch. Concerning this leper, disregarding the law of man, Jesus reached out and he touched him. (Matthew 8:9–13)

The people I know who love like Jesus are in the habit of physically touching those they love. And they're on the lookout for those who will be encouraged by their touch.

Jesus' touch accomplished great things in the leper.

Your touch can accomplish great things too.

Love like Jesus did.

Touch.

Notes:
1. Benedict Carey, "Evidence That Little Touches Do Mean So Much," *New York Times*, 2/22/2010

- Joe & Cindy Pike - Deb's friends
- Rey & Carrie - Austin
- My family - Issues
- Pecco's Mom
- Shawn - new friend
- Taylor - newer

CHAPTER 6

Love Like Jesus

Love the Lost Cause

Now there is in Jerusalem by the Sheep Gate a pool, in Aramaic called Bethesda, which has five roofed colonnades. In these lay a multitude of invalids—blind, lame, and paralyzed. One man was there who had been an invalid for thirty-eight years. When Jesus saw him lying there and knew that he had already been there a long time, he said to him, "Do you want to be healed?" The sick man answered him, "Sir, I have no one to put me into the pool when the water is stirred up, and while I am going another steps down before me." Jesus said to him, "Get up, take your bed, and walk." And at once the man was healed, and he took up his bed and walked.

JOHN 5:2–9

Daniel's Decline and Nate's Devotion

My son Nate has a heart for those people who others have dismissed as a lost cause. Today he told me about a disabled man he cared for in an adult foster home. The disabled man's name is Daniel. Daniel is angry all the time, and he can't speak or do much of anything to take care of himself. After working there for a while,

Nate was surprised to learn, up until five years previously, Daniel was happy, and could speak and communicate very well. But over time the level of engagement with Daniel gradually declined, and so his communication skills and function declined also, until he became the sad figure he is today. Nate felt like the caregivers saw Daniel's disability and wrote him off as someone not worth engaging. But Jesus didn't see people that way. Even those who were disabled.

How Jesus Loved People

Jesus loved the disabled man lying at the pool of Bethesda, even though anyone else would have considered him a lost cause.

Some ancient manuscripts explain the system in place here at the pool of Bethesda. The disabled people would get up and enter the pool whenever they saw the water move, or swirl, or bubble. Tradition said the first one in the pool after the waters moved would be healed.

In our culture, we also have a system. Like the system at the pool of Bethesda, our system is also a system of competition. Just as it was at the pool of Bethesda, in our system, the rewards go to the person who is first. My own tendency, probably because of my own competitive nature, is to help those who help themselves. My tendency is to help those who, in my estimation, have a shot at making it into the pool first, so to speak.

But that's not Christ's way. Jesus loves the lost cause.

How to Love Like Jesus

There's a great movie that illustrates the way Jesus loved people others would call a lost cause. It's called *Temple Grandin*—it's the true story of an autistic girl of the same name. Temple didn't speak until she was almost four years old. She was diagnosed with autism, and the specialists who examined her wrote her off. They recommended her mother place Temple in an institution. But her mother didn't listen to the doctors. She kept her at home and taught Temple with amazing perseverance and tenacity.

Incredibly, Temple eventually earned her Ph.D., and at the time of this writing, she's a professor of Animal Science at Colorado State University.

Temple Grandin's mother had no education, no training, no anything to help her with her daughter. The only thing she had was her love for Temple. And that love was so strong, she single-handedly revolutionized the approach to treating children with autism and Asperger's.[1]

Jesus chose to help a man who had lived with a disability for *thirty-eight years*; that's a long time without change or improvement. Jesus chose to help a man who had no one else to help him. Jesus chose to help a man who was at the back of the pack, who was helpless to win the competition to be the first into the water to be healed.

Jesus loved a lost cause.

Oh, how I've blown it with the lost causes in my life. When I see someone who, in my estimation, is a lost cause, I can only think of one word to describe my attitude toward that person, and the word is not *love*.

The word is *dismissive*.

I dismiss those who I determine to be beyond help. I dismiss the man in my neighborhood traveling the streets in his motorized wheelchair. I dismiss the disabled woman who collects bottles and cans around town for the deposit money. God have mercy on me,

I dismiss them.

But Christ does not.

And I have that attitude even though there have been times in my life when I was dismissed as a lost cause. But Jesus did not dismiss me.

The man in our story lived with a disability for thirty-eight years. Yet he was the one chosen by Jesus.

You and I may not have the power to command someone with a disability to pick up his mat and walk. But there's nothing stopping us from loving that person. Just taking the time to engage a disabled person with whatever help we can offer, even if it's just an accepting and loving conversation, can make a big difference in his or her life. Just offering a ride to church to anyone in the lost-cause category could be a big deal.

Jesus loved lost causes.

The people I know who are successful at loving like Jesus find a way to love those who appear to be lost causes. Sometimes they love in big ways, oftentimes in small ways.

But they don't dismiss them.

Notes
1. "Temple Grandin," IMDb.com, 2010

- Delaney - cancer - 14 yrs old
- Kevin
- Jared - baptized
- Jen - cough
- Taylor - nauseau

CHAPTER 7

Love Like Jesus

Give Like Jesus

. . . he said to Simon, "Put out into the deep and let down your nets for a catch." And Simon answered, "Master, we toiled all night and took nothing! But at your word I will let down the nets." And when they had done this, they enclosed a large number of fish, and their nets were breaking. They signaled to their partners in the other boat to come and help them. And they came and filled both the boats, so that they began to sink. But when Simon Peter saw it, he fell down at Jesus' knees, saying, "Depart from me, for I am a sinful man, O Lord." For he and all who were with him were astonished at the catch of fish that they had taken . . . And Jesus said to Simon, "Do not be afraid; from now on you will be catching men." And when they had brought their boats to land, they left everything and followed him.

LUKE 5:4–11

How Jesus Loved People

Jesus gave so generously that the recipients were astonished. And he gave in a way that engendered a certain response: In our passage for this chapter, Peter responds by recognizing the glory of Jesus and his own sinful nature. And they all respond by leaving everything, and following Jesus.

How to Love Like Jesus

Jesus gave in a way that attracted people to God, and inspired people to glorify God. But do you suppose I give of myself that way? When I give materially, or when I give my time, or when I give my energy, do I do it in a way that encourages people to glorify God and follow Jesus? Too often the answer is no.

Too frequently I give in a way that I hope will encourage people to follow *me.*

Most of us give out of a desire to attract people to ourselves. We say to ourselves, "If I help him move, he'll think I'm a good guy." Or, "If I pick up the check, he'll think I'm generous." Or, "If I make a great dessert, they'll think I'm a great cook." It's human nature to think this way.

But everything you and I have is God's anyway. Nothing is your own. Your money, your time, your energy, your talents and abilities, your life: they're all His. You and I are just managing what we've received from Him. It only makes sense then that you and I should manage His gifts in a way that draws people closer to God and to His Son.

This conflict between giving to attract followers to ourselves versus giving to attract followers to Jesus is relevant to anyone on social media, or anyone who blogs or tweets or speaks or writes for God's kingdom. When we look at our number of friends or followers or subscribers or page views, are we looking out of an interest in drawing people closer to Christ? If you are, that's a good thing. Jesus advocated numbering the one hundred so the shepherd knew he was missing the one. Tracking numbers out of concern for gathering sheep to Christ's sheepfold is good. But we're in error when we track numbers out of a desire to see how *our* followers have grown. You could say it's Matthew 18:12 vs. 2 Samuel 24.

Looking at his numbers to gratify himself was what David did when he numbered the men in his army. *But David's heart struck him after he had numbered the people. And David said to the Lord, "I have sinned greatly in what I have done. But now, O Lord, please take away the iniquity of your servant, for I have done very foolishly."* (2 Samuel 24)

A positive example is Jeremiah, the weeping prophet. He preached for forty-two years, and not one person responded. But while I'm sure he would have been encouraged to see people respond, he didn't give of himself that way for people. He gave of himself that way for God. Was it worth it? In the gospels and the New Testament Jeremiah is quoted ten times. Anytime you give anything, it's important for you to ask yourself the question, "Am I doing this so people will think well of me, am I doing this so people will follow me? Or am I doing it so people will follow Jesus Christ?"

I hear people say they want to be inspired by God's Holy Spirit when they create. Whatever it is—their blog post, or their music, or their movie, or their book, or their culinary creation—they desire inspiration. I know I certainly want that. If you're like me and want the Holy Spirit's inspiration, it's important to remember the purpose of the Holy Spirit is to glorify Jesus Christ. (John 16:13–14)

The people I know who love like Jesus, and receive God's inspiration in the greatest measure, give in the context of unmistakable love. When we're filled with God's love for someone and filled with love for God, our desire to make ourselves look good disappears. It's then that the Holy Spirit moves. It's then our giving glorifies God and draws people closer to Christ.

Speaking of the Holy Spirit, Jesus said,

> *He will not speak on his own . . . he will glorify me . . .*
> *John 16:13–14*

41

- John's ribs
- Joe Pike — blood circulation
  to brain

CHAPTER 8

Love Like Jesus

Don't Love Everyone the Same

*And he allowed no one to follow him except Peter
and James and John the brother of James.*
MARK 5:37

How Jesus Loved People

Jesus loved everybody, but he didn't love everybody the same. Have you ever thought about that? He loved (and loves) every person on the planet. He loves every one of us so much, he laid down his life, for each of us. But when he was here, walking the earth, he loved different people differently. He fed five thousand, then four thousand, for a total of nine thousand, but he didn't feed everybody. The people he fed were those who followed him and listened to him. He didn't heal everybody. The people he healed were the ones who believed in him and cried out to him. He didn't train everybody.

He trained seventy-two of his closest followers as his ambassadors. (Luke 10) And then there's the twelve.

There were twelve who were especially close to him. He let them in, close, so they could see up close how he lived.

He gave the twelve private insights into parables left unexplained to others. (Mark 4:10) And then there's the three: Peter, James, and John. Jesus let these three in even closer. He loved Peter, James, and John by bringing them with him for the transfiguration; and when he raised Jairus' daughter from the dead; and when he sweat great drops of blood in the garden of Gethsemane just before they took him away to be tried and sentenced to crucifixion in their corrupt court system. Only the three were allowed to accompany Jesus during those occasions. (Matthew 17:1–11, Mark 5:35–43, Mark 14:32–52)

How to Love Like Jesus

Before Jesus chose the twelve, he spent the night on a mountainside praying about who he should choose. (Luke 6:12–16) To love like Jesus, you do the same. Prayerfully seek out who your Father will have you love, like Jesus loved the three, and the twelve, and the seventy-two, and the nine thousand. For many of us, those closest three will be family members. The twelve might be other family, neighbors, and co-workers. The seventy-two might be more neighbors and co-workers. And the thousands might be people you reach on social media. For some of us, instead of three, there may only be one, and instead of the twelve, there may only be—another one. And that's it. Most of us will fall somewhere in between. Take comfort in knowing that you, like John the Baptist, are not the Christ. So don't feel like you have to minister to thousands as Jesus did, or even a dozen, like Jesus did. (John 1:20)

It's not how many that's important, prayerfully choosing is what's important. Prayer is the key. Jesus prayerfully chose the twelve. And not one of those twelve belonged to the Levitical priesthood. In fact, none were remarkable in any way. Their only common traits were their desire to follow Jesus and learn. Prayerfully finding people with those traits is important. Asking your Father to lead you to choose people who love Jesus, desire to follow him closely and learn, as those to let in closest, and asking your Father to lead you in choosing who to let in less, can result in the abundant life He wants for you. (John 15:11) But moving forward without your Father's direction will result in a depleted life. There were times in *my* life when I made friends without praying or thinking. I made friends mostly based on who I seemed to click with. During those times my life was random and unfruitful at best, dark and sinful at worst. Other people I observe who make friends this way have similar outcomes.

How Jesus Loved Those He Let in Close, and How You Can Too

Billy Graham once said:

> *Christ, I think, set the pattern. He spent most of his time with twelve men. He didn't spend it with a great crowd. In fact, every time he had a great crowd it seems to me that there weren't too many results. The great results, it seems to me, came in this personal interview and in the time he spent with his twelve.*[1]

When we look at how Jesus loved people differently, and how he loved those he let in close, we see a pattern emerge. It's a pattern you and I can adopt ourselves. You can love those you let in close the way Jesus loved those he let in close. When Jesus called John and Andrew, he invited them to "come and see." (John 1:39)

~ So let the ones you let in close come and see how you live. Let them see your intimate walk with Jesus. Model the life of a true Christ follower as Jesus was a model to his disciples. Let them hear you pray, as Jesus let those he let in close hear him pray. Let them hear scripture in your conversation, even as Jesus' disciples heard scripture in Jesus' conversation. Let them see how you live out what you learn from this book, and more importantly, how you live out what you learn from the scriptures.

~ Then, after a time, ask those you let in close to assist you in doing the work of God's kingdom. Ask them to assist you in ministry as Jesus asked his disciples to assist him in ministry.

~ Then *you* help them do ministry for a time. Give them an outlet. If there's no outlet for them, like a pond without its water flowing, stagnation is the certain result.

~ Then let them work alone. And then they can reproduce the pattern.

Remember, Jesus' intention all along was for those closest to him to produce his likeness in others. Bearing fruit was and is essential to following Christ. The branch must bear fruit. (John 15:1–2) This was the pattern we saw from Jesus in his relationships with those closest to him, the twelve, and even the seventy-two. And the disciples learned this pattern because Jesus let them in.

Robert E. Coleman puts it this way:

Having called his men, Jesus made a practice of being with them. This was the essence of his training program—just letting his disciples follow him.

When one stops to think of it, this was an incredibly simple way of doing it. Jesus had no formal school, no seminaries, no outlined courses of study, no periodic membership classes in which he enrolled his followers. None of these highly organized procedures considered so necessary today entered into his ministry. Amazing as it may seem, all Jesus did to teach these men his way was to draw them close to himself.[1]

This is how Jesus loved people, he loved different people differently. He loved all people, but he didn't love all people the same. For Jesus, there was a steep increase in priority from the masses to those he was most intimate with.

And the greatest fruit came from the few he let in close.

The people I know who love like Jesus don't love everyone the same. They're prayerfully intentional about who they let in close, and who they have contact with more occasionally. They prayerfully choose to let a small number in close, even as Jesus did.

Then they love those they let in close, the way Jesus loved those he let in close.

When Jesus called John and Andrew, he invited them to "come and see."
John 1:39

Notes:
1. Robert E. Coleman, *The Master Plan of Evangelism*, Revell, 1993

Further study will be rewarded. I recommend Robert E. Coleman's classic: *The Master Plan of Evangelism*, and David and Paul Watson's excellent book, *Contagious Disciple Making*. Much of what you've read in this chapter came from or was inspired by those two sources.
David Watson and Paul Watson, *Contagious Disciple Making: Leading Others on a Journey of Discovery*, Thomas Nelson, 2014

11-17

- VA students
- Jared buys a house!
- Alex - surgery appendicitis
- Safe return - OS + prly Tom
- John sister - cancer
          & Maria
- Scan - results from VA
- Taylor - morning sickness

CHAPTER 9

Love Like Jesus

Pray Like Jesus

Trapped

"The Grange," as the locals called it, was a large retail store and warehouse that sold agricultural supplies on South Pacific Highway in Medford, Oregon. It was on fire. Right around 3:00 a.m., Bob Paulson and two of his crewmates dragged a hoseline through an open bay door and disappeared into the thick black smoke. Because of that smoke they could see only a few feet in front of them. So they were feeling their way, peering through the darkness, looking for any sign of light from the flames that waited for them inside. Everything was typical of a commercial structure fire so far, with one exception: The flames they were looking for couldn't be found. They could feel the heat, there was dense smoke, but they couldn't locate the source.

Because he had only been on the department one year, it was Bob's job to operate the nozzle. He was first through the door and he would be the last one out. He and two other firefighters dragged the two-and-one-half-inch diameter hoseline along a path that resembled the letter J. After working their way 150 feet deep into the structure, and still finding no flames, they decided to retreat back outside. In a zero-visibility situation such as this, firefighters are trained to follow the hose back out of the building, but Bob thought he could take a shortcut across the hook of the J. So he dropped the nozzle, headed through the pitch-dark smoke for what he thought was the way out. He didn't make it far. After a few moments, he bumped into a wall. "Not good," he thought to himself. He turned around and headed back in the general direction of the hoseline, but somehow he missed it.

"By now I was totally disoriented," Bob said. "I had no idea which way to go."

He felt his way along until he found a large roll-up door, but it had a padlock on it. It was around this time the low-air warning bell started ringing on his breathing apparatus.

"So my low-air bell's going off, and the roll-up doors had these little narrow 4" x 12" windows in them," Bob said. "I'm looking through them to the outside, but I can't see anybody."

Then he found another roll-up door next to the first one, but it, too, was padlocked. Then he found a third roll-up door, but that one was padlocked also. He thought about trying to break one of the windows so he could stick his air hose out into the relatively clean air. But he couldn't find anything to use to break the glass. Anyway, he couldn't stand the thought of just standing there, with his air hose out the window, waiting for the fire to consume him.

It was all too much. He could feel the panic start to rise inside. Then, behind him, he just barely made out the sound of someone else's low-air warning bell, off in the distance. Because his own bell was ringing so loudly, it was difficult to tell where the sound of the other bell was coming from.

He thought about trying to follow that sound, that other bell. But if he stayed where he was, at least he had a window. Maybe someone would walk by and see him. On the other hand, even if someone did walk by and see him, they might not be able to force the door before he ran out of air. And as soon as he runs out of air, he's dead. But, if he left the bay door, he was giving up his one point of reference and venturing into the unknown. All he knew about moving toward the interior was it would be hotter, and blacker, than where he was now.

In the end, he decided to take a chance, and follow the sound of the bell.

After his ordeal, Bob described his narrow escape by saying, "Through the Lord's guidance, no brilliance of my own, I came walking out [of the building], about fifteen feet behind Finnegan." (Finnegan was Bob's crewmate.)[1]

How Jesus Loved People
Jesus prayed for the people he loved. He prayed for Peter to be delivered from Satan, he prayed for his friend Lazarus' resurrection, he prayed while he hung on the cross for those who put him there, he prayed for his disciples. (Luke 22:31–32, John 11:41–42, Luke 23:34, John 17:6–19)

He even prayed for those who would believe because of his disciples, which means he prayed for you, and he prayed for me. (John 17:20–23)

Jesus loved people by praying for them.

The Curious Case of Edna Hahnsdorf
I don't know about you, but there are times when I become discouraged in prayer. It just feels like I've been praying for something forever, without results. Or it feels like I'm praying to an imaginary friend.

Or it feels like my prayers aren't going anywhere, as if the wings of my prayers have been clipped somehow and they aren't even getting off the ground. When you feel this way you might be tempted to think prayer is just a waste of time; but before you make up your mind, you might want to consider the last part of Bob Paulson's nearly fatal fire story.

At the end of my interview with Bob, he said, "Three days after the fire I saw my Aunt Edna, Edna Hahnsdorf, and she asked me, 'Where were you early in the morning on Thursday? Because the Lord woke me up at three in the morning on that day, and said: "Pray for Bob." After praying for you about a half hour, I thought, 'OK, whatever it was is OK,' and I went back to sleep.'"

And that Thursday morning was October 30, the time and date of the Grange fire, when, as Bob puts it, "I was reasonably sure I was going to die."

Why Did Jesus Pray?

It's easy to see why Edna prayed. She knew her nephew Bob was a firefighter and that he could find himself in harm's way. And during the early morning hours when Bob was lost in the fire, she was somehow prompted by God's Holy Spirit to pray for the nephew she loved. But why did Jesus pray? Have you ever wondered?

Why would Jesus, God incarnate Himself, why would He ever pray? I mean, Jesus is the Son of God. He's the Alpha and the Omega.

But He still prayed.

Why?

Love—and Something Surprising

Part of the answer is Jesus was communicating with the One he loved more than any other. The One with whom he had a relationship from the beginning of eternity. And any good relationship requires good communication. But there's another reason: Jesus also prayed because He could do nothing without his Father. And He said so.

Jesus Christ, God's only begotten Son, said, "I can do nothing on my own." (John 5:30) Jesus Christ, the Messiah and Savior of the world said, "Truly, truly, I say to you, the Son can do nothing of his own accord." (John 5:19) And he also said, ". . . the Father who dwells in me does his works." (John 14:10)

Think about that attitude for a minute. And then think about your own attitude. Jesus Christ lived life in an attitude of dependency on our Father. I don't know about you, but for most of my life, I lived in an attitude of self-sufficiency.

And an attitude of self-sufficiency encourages a life without prayer.

How to Love Like Jesus

Bob's story makes me wonder what might have happened had his Aunt Edna ignored the Holy Spirit's promptings and rolled over and gone back to sleep—without praying. I wonder if Bob would have made it. And that makes me wonder about my own prayers. Who might be saved, and who might perish, depending on whether or not I'm responding to the promptings of God's Holy Spirit? And how might I be held accountable, for ignoring those promptings?

The people I know who love like Jesus, pray like Jesus. They respond to the Holy Spirit's promptings to pray.

They pray even if it interrupts their sleep, at 3:00 a.m.

They pray for those they love because Jesus prayed for those he loved.

Prayers make a difference.

Your prayers will make a difference.

Just ask Bob Paulson.

Notes:
1. Interview with Medford Fire Captain Bob Paulson, August 24, 2013

Further study will be rewarded. Read John 17:6–26 to see how Jesus prayed for his disciples and how he prayed for you and for me.

The Grange Co-op Fire:
Firefighter Bennington, commenting on the fire's size and intensity, said, "If God himself told me to go back in there, I wouldn't have gone."
After the roof collapse, Finnegan and Paulson entered back into the building where they encountered Battalion Chief Ryan Johnson. He was ordering all fire personnel to evacuate. Finnegan asked for one more minute to fight the fire. The Batt Chief gave him three. Finnegan and Paulson found the fire and extinguished it.

CHAPTER 10

Love Like Jesus

No Family or Rich Friends

When you give a dinner or a banquet, do not invite your friends or your brothers or your relatives or rich neighbors, lest they also invite you in return and you be repaid. But when you give a feast, invite the poor, the crippled, the lame, the blind, and you will be blessed, because they cannot repay you. For you will be repaid at the resurrection of the just.

LUKE 14:12–14

Kids at Their Table

There's an old joke about a couple who couldn't have kids. They sought the help of their pastor who said he would fast and pray the last day of every month until they conceived. Shortly thereafter the couple moved to another town, so the couple and the pastor lost touch.

After a year of fasting in this fashion, the pastor ran into the woman who couldn't have kids. He asked if anything happened and she shared they had a set of triplets; and not only that but she was twelve weeks pregnant; and not only *that* but her doctor said she might be pregnant with twins. The pastor was overjoyed. He asked where her husband was so he could find him and congratulate him. She said,

"He's been gone for a week now, looking for you—he's bringing you food!"

That story reminds me of my barber, Don. Don and his wife Jan just seem to accumulate kids. But it hasn't happened through procreation. They have two of their own biological children, and then beyond that, I've lost count—and I'm not kidding. He and his wife took in foster child after foster child. Along the way they somehow wound up adopting a large assortment of those foster children. The stories he tells me about his family while I'm sitting in that barber's chair are pretty crazy. Some of the kids they adopted have serious issues.

What they've given to those kids, though, those kids can never pay back.

How Jesus Loved People

Jesus loved people by giving what could never be repaid. Not only did he heal and help people who couldn't repay him while he was here on earth, but he gave you and he gave me what can't be repaid too. He was (and is) royalty. He is God's only begotten Son. He was with God in the beginning. And he made everything. So what could anyone possibly give that would serve as repayment to Jesus? And how could we ever repay him for what he did for us on the cross? (John 1:1–4)

Love Like Jesus

This idea of loving people who can't repay is one of the most important concepts in our quest to love like Jesus. We sometimes think of the miracles Jesus performed, throw up our hands and say, "Compared to Christ, what could I ever do for anyone?" But the reality is, there are plenty of people you can bless who can't return the favor. There are people who would be thrilled just to have a few minutes of your attention, or a few dollars from your wallet, or a few morsels of your food.

Maybe you're like me. Maybe most of the love you show people is toward those who *can* repay you. My lunch and dinner table is most often filled with friends and family who are likely to invite me back. And, quite often, when I give to someone who is likely to repay me—I'm proud of myself for doing it! I dwell on what I've given, and don't give much thought to the probable payback.

But to love like Jesus, you and I need to seek out and give to the poor, the crippled, the lame, the blind, and the kids. That's how we'll be blessed. As Jesus said, although they can't repay us, we'll be repaid at the resurrection of the just.

The people I know who love like Jesus, find those who aren't capable of reciprocating.

They find them and love them.

They give to them what they can never repay.

That's how Jesus loved people.

That's how we can love like Jesus.

For if you love those who love you, what reward do you have?
Do not even the tax collectors do the same?
Matthew 5:46

- Pluger-fact + unimportant
  ↳ margin died
- poor, homeless, elderly, alone
- powerless

121

CHAPTER 11

Love Like Jesus

Heal Like Jesus

*People brought all their sick to him and begged
him to let the sick just touch the edge of his cloak,
and all who touched it were healed.*
MATTHEW 14:35–36 (NIV)

How Jesus Loved People

People from all around brought their sick to Jesus, and everyone who touched the edge of his cloak was healed.

I did a search on the definition of a *cloak*, and this was the first thing that came up: *An outdoor overgarment, typically sleeveless, that hangs from the shoulders.*

That confirmed what I already suspected,

I don't even own a cloak.

And if I did, anyone who touched it wouldn't be healed.

In contrast to an average Joe like me, Jesus healed all manner of sickness. He healed lepers (once he healed ten at a time), paralytics, people with withered hands, bleeding women, blind men, dying children, and epileptics. He healed deaf men, women with fevers, and he reattached severed body parts. He even raised people from the dead.

Jesus favored healing people by touching them. Occasionally he healed remotely; by just saying it would happen, it happened. He preferred to heal instantaneously, as opposed to progressively. He liked to heal totally and completely, as opposed to partial healing.

Jesus loved people, by healing them.

How to Love Like Jesus

My wife Kathy is a great example of how someone without a cloak can heal people. When our grandson Andrew was nine months old, he had a deformity of his skull called Bilateral Isolated Frontosphenoidal Craniosynostosis. That's a fancy medical term that means the part of Andrew's skull behind his eyes and around his left temple wasn't growing and expanding as fast as the rest of his skull. Without surgical intervention, the left frontal lobe of his brain might not have enough room to grow properly. The surgery was complicated and involved folding down Andrew's face and removing the front part of his skull, including the forehead. But the left frontal lobe is the part of the brain that provides our speech and language function. So no intervention could compromise Andrew's ability to talk, read, and write.

The required surgery was expensive and involved travel. The hospital where the procedure would be performed was Phoenix Children's Hospital, in Phoenix, Arizona, a thousand miles away from our home in Oregon.

So Kathy organized a massive garage sale to raise money for the cause. She also arranged for us to travel with our son, daughter-in-law, and grandson to provide support in Arizona. After the surgery, Kathy was over at our son and daughter-in-law's almost every day. She did anything she could to help with the healing process.

Fast-forward eighteen months: As I write this, my daughter-in-law is on our couch downstairs recovering from a broken foot. She broke her foot while chasing a very healthy and energetic two-year-old Andrew because Andrew is now healed. And Kathy is helping to heal again. She's helping Andrew's mother with the healing of a broken foot. She's watching Andrew, and serving our daughter-in-law food, and putting ice on her foot, and driving her to the doctor's office, and doing anything and everything she can to help the healing process. She's healing by touching, she's touching the life of Charise, our daughter-in-law.

And while all that's going on, Kathy's on the phone with doctors and relatives, helping an older family member (who lives in Chicago, two thousand miles away) negotiate the process of major oral surgery. So she's also healing remotely, if you will.

I'm not saying there aren't people who can heal miraculously, like Jesus did. I'm just saying that so far, I'm not one of them. Maybe you're like me. Maybe you don't own a cloak, and even if you did, if someone touched it, they wouldn't be healed anyway. But that's OK. There's plenty you can do to help the healing process. Next time your neighbor, or your friend, or your family member needs healing, instead of focusing on what you can't do, focus on what you can do, then do everything you can, to help the healing process.

Do everything you can, to help them heal.

That's how Jesus loved people.

That's how you can love like Jesus.

1-12

- Debbie - Last Day
- Uncle Lonnie
- Praise - Bill's Surgery
- Deb's sibling - died
- Bethy - Back surgery
  (Bruce's Dghtr)
- Kelli - Neck Pain
- Deb - Hip pain

CHAPTER 12

Love Like Jesus

Even if It Disrupts Your Sabbath

*Jesus said to the man with the shriveled hand,
"Stand up in front of everyone."
Then Jesus asked them, "Which is lawful on the
Sabbath: to do good or to do evil, to save life
or to kill?" But they remained silent.
He looked around at them in anger and, deeply dis-
tressed at their stubborn hearts, said to the man,
"Stretch out your hand." He stretched it out,
and his hand was completely restored.*
MARK 3:3–6

How Jesus Loved People

Jesus cared more about loving the man with the withered hand than he did about keeping the Pharisees' tradition concerning the Sabbath.

How to Love Like Jesus

She was walking on the shoulder of the road, in bare feet, on a day when it was too cold to be out in bare feet. Her mascara ran in the shape of a capital "U" down both cheeks. She was crying. No, she was sobbing.

Kathy and I were on our way to our church. The drive takes you through the beautiful mountains between the Rogue and Applegate valleys. The church I was attending at that time is an amazing place. It's an example of how God can do anything He wants to do, anywhere He wants to do it. Because our church at the time was in a beautiful but remote location, yet every week thousands traveled there to attend services. It doesn't make any sense. There's no human logic to it. The teaching and the worship are outstanding, and I could hardly stand to miss a service.

I could hardly stand to miss a service but . . . but this lady who was in obvious distress. What would God have us do?

What We Did

Kathy and I fired up a quick prayer, turned around, and offered her a ride. As we listened, we learned she was crying because she just left an abusive boyfriend who had done her harm. She was barefoot because she left in a hurry. After hearing her story, we asked her if we could pray for her. She said yes, so we did.

There was no way she could return home, so we took her to her friend's house about fifteen miles away from our church.

We missed our visit to God's house that day. But I believe we were led by the Holy Spirit to do precisely what God wanted us to do, and to be precisely where God wanted us to be on that Sunday morning. During the ride over to her friend's, we encouraged her to go to our church. And over the next several weeks we saw her there, receiving counseling from pastors.

I just heard it said a few days ago, "Human need trumps religious creed. Love trumps the law." Jesus expressed love to people when his Sabbath was disrupted, when his teaching was interrupted, when his prayers were disrupted, and when his travels were interrupted. (Mark 1:21–26, 35–39, 40–42) When Jesus' Sabbath was disrupted, and when Jesus was interrupted in general, he responded by loving people.

"Which is lawful on the Sabbath: to do good or to do evil?" Jesus asked, rhetorically.

He's telling you, and telling me:

It's good to do good on the Sabbath.

Jesus loved people, even when it meant disrupting *his* Sabbath. Bob Goff put it this way. He wrote, "Loving people the way Jesus did means living a life filled with constant interruptions." When I did the deep dive into Jesus' life, that's exactly what I found. Jesus loved people when it disrupted his Sabbath: or his prayer, or his teaching, or his travels, or, it would seem, anytime he was interrupted.[1]

You and I can love like Jesus by helping someone, even if it means disrupting *your* Sabbath. When your Sabbath's disrupted, or when you're interrupted for any reason, thank God for the interruption and ask Him: "Where's the opportunity to express Jesus' love in this?"

A Word about the Sabbath Rhythm

I feel compelled to add this word of caution because today, most people discount the Sabbath, if they don't ignore it completely. That's not the rhythm God has in mind for you or for me. There's a balance here. It's clear from the gospels, Jesus lived in God's rhythm of the Sabbath. What Jesus did in chapter 3 of Mark stands out because he did something out of the ordinary. What we can learn from Jesus healing the man with the withered hand is not that we should ignore the Sabbath and engage in work every day. What we can learn is we're not to use the Sabbath (or anything else) as a reason *not* to act on the Holy Spirit's leading to engage people with Jesus' love.

> *Above all, keep loving one another earnestly . . .*
> *1 Peter 4:8*

Notes:
1. Bob Goff, @bobgoff, Twitter, April 10, 2019

CHAPTER 13

Love Like Jesus

Calm the Storm

And a great windstorm arose, and the waves were breaking into the boat, so that the boat was already fill-ing. But he was in the stern, asleep on the cushion. And they woke him and said to him, "Teacher, do you not care that we are perishing?" And he awoke and rebuked the wind and said to the sea, "Peace! Be still!" And the wind ceased, and there was a great calm.

MARK 4:37–39

A Storm Hits a Wedding Ceremony

I went to this wedding once where the person who took charge of planning the event had a beautiful vision for it. It was going to happen outside, and it was going to be done in a very particular way so as to make the setting spectacular. The only thing was, the entire plan was geared for the outdoors. It was arranged to happen outside, so the wedding and reception depended on dry, calm weather. And whenever the person in charge of the wedding was asked what she would do if it rained, she simply said: It won't rain.

Well, guess what?

A storm arose, and it rained.

And the weather outside wasn't the only storm that day. With no indoor venue or arrangements made whatsoever, the wedding planner just shut down. Panic ensued as the bride, the bride's mother, and many others frantically attempted to pull something together.

Then in stepped a few people who were friends of the bride's mother. In a very gentle and gracious manner they just sort of took over. They found a gym they could use at a Christian high school. They figured out how to arrange the outdoor tables and chairs to accommodate the guests, even though the gym was a much smaller venue than expected. They found a place for the caterer to set up. They improvised with the decorations designed for the outdoors. They were amazing.

It wasn't long after this small group of people engaged the problem that the storm subsided and a calm came over the bride and the rest of the wedding party.

How Jesus Loved People

When the disciples took Jesus across the sea of Galilee, and the storm came, there was panic. The disciples in the boat were terror-stricken—because of a storm—so Jesus calmed it.

How to Love Like Jesus

Jesus loved the disciples by calming their storm. You and I can't command the wind and the waves, but there are other storms we *can* calm.

Just like Jesus, God has put you in a boat with a group of people. They're the ones in your family, in your workplace, in your circle of friends. And just like the disciples in the boat, they'll experience storms. And sometimes, like the friends of the bride's mother at the wedding, you'll have the power to calm those storms.

When someone you know is panicked, maybe you're just the right person to bring them peace. Maybe their storm is a computer that's down, or a car that won't start, or the end of a relationship, or the loss of a job.

You just might be uniquely qualified to calm the wind and the waves.

Jesus calmed the storm for his disciples.

The people I know who love like Jesus look for opportunities to calm storms. When they see someone who's panicked, they engage the problem. And they calm their storm.

That's how Jesus loved people.

That's how you can love like Jesus.

- Pearce's Niece
- Oliver - MRI - Feb. 27
    ' Tumors
- Maria - Uterus, Ovaries

CHAPTER 14

Love Like Jesus

Forgiveness and Paralysis

And behold, some people brought to him a paralytic, lying on a bed. And when Jesus saw their faith, he said to the paralytic, "Take heart, my son; your sins are forgiven." And behold, some of the scribes said to themselves, "This man is blaspheming." But Jesus, knowing their thoughts, said, "Why do you think evil in your hearts? For which is easier, to say, 'Your sins are forgiven,' or to say, 'Rise and walk'? But that you may know that the Son of Man has authority on earth to forgive sins"—he then said to the paralytic—"Rise, pick up your bed and go home." And he rose and went home.
MATTHEW 9:2–7

How Jesus Loved People

Jesus loved the paralytic by forgiving him.

How to Love Like Jesus
Years ago I was a one-man information technology team for the fire department where I worked. My primary job was that of a firefighter, but

in the evenings at the fire station, and on my days off at headquarters, I would purchase computers, install software, and program databases.

As the de facto department expert, I often had co-workers ask me questions about their personal computer purchases. I remember one time my friend, Frank Finnegan, asked me if he should buy a PC or a Mac. I explained—in a most eloquent manner—how the PC is less expensive, and how you can right click, and why it has more flexibility if you want to upgrade, and how there's a bigger selection of software available.

Frank patiently listened to my brilliant and detailed explanation, nodding to indicate his understanding and agreement.

Then he went out and bought a Mac.

I was so mad. It doesn't make any sense whatsoever, but I felt completely betrayed. Things were strained between us, and for a ridiculous reason. For months I was stuck, I was bound, I was frozen in my relationship with my good friend Frank.

I was paralyzed.

I wonder if God in His wisdom purposely included forgiveness and paralysis in the same passage of scripture. Because when you can't let go, when you can't show grace, when you can't release your anger and resentment—when you can't forgive, you become paralyzed.

I was paralyzed in my friendship with Frank, and I've observed many others whose lives were paralyzed by unforgiveness too. The woman with tremendous potential who remains in poverty because she's overwhelmed with anger toward her parents. The negotiator who can't come to agreement because he won't forgive the union president. The woman who heard what was said behind her back, and can't let it go.

They're paralyzed by their unforgiveness. And they're paralyzed in their ability to love like Jesus.

There's a great article in USA Today about what makes people happy. A statement from that article by University of Michigan psychologist Christopher Peterson stands out and is relevant to our discussion in this chapter about how Jesus loved people. The statement is this: "Forgiveness is the trait most strongly linked to happiness."[1]

Forgiveness.

Forgiveness, forgiveness, forgiveness. No wonder Jesus emphasized it so. His desire is for us to enter into a big, abundant life, walking with him here on earth, and dwelling with him later in heaven. (John 10:10) To live that abundant life on earth, he tells us, we must learn to forgive. (Matthew 6:14, 18:21–22, 18:23–35, Mark 11:25)

Do you want to love like Jesus, unencumbered? Do you want to be free from anger, resentment, and disappointment? And do you want to be happy? Then learn to forgive. Forgive everyone, of everything. Forgive 77 times. (Matthew 18:21–22)

Jesus loved people by forgiving, he forgave the paralytic, he forgave the woman who anointed him at dinner, and he forgave us all when he hung there, dying, on the cross. (Matthew 9:2–7, Luke 7:48, Luke 23:34)

So don't allow paralysis to get in the way of loving like Jesus.

To love like Jesus, forgive.

You're the one who will be blessed if you do.

Notes:

1. University of Michigan psychologist Christopher Peterson in an article by Marilyn Elias, "Psychologists now know what makes people happy," USA TODAY, 12/8/2002, URL: http://usatoday30.usatoday.com/news/health/2002-12-08-happy-main_x.htm

1-26

- Ddy A + B
- Paul - No Stroke
- Deb's hip
- Multi MRI
- Betty - No Blood Clots
- Delaney
- Holly - Colonoscopy
- Ostoluats - Travel

CHAPTER 15

Love Like Jesus

Open the Door to Heaven

*But woe to you, scribes and Pharisees, hypocrites! For you
shut the kingdom of heaven in people's faces. For you neither
enter yourselves nor allow those who would enter to go in.*

MATTHEW 23:13

Battles on Social Media

Social media is in its usual tumultuous state. My Republican friends
are attacking a prominent Democrat. And my Democrat friends
are attacking a prominent Republican.

All this back and forth has me thinking about the traditional
positions of both my liberal and conservative friends, and how it
might affect our door-keeping—as in opening or shutting the door
of heaven, and how my big opinions can have a way of slamming
that door closed.

A nightmare of mine is that on the day of judgment, *my* day of judgment, after I die, I stand before God, and He says the words: You're guilty, of shutting the door of the kingdom of heaven in people's faces.

Father in heaven, let me never hear those words.

Jesus chastised the Pharisees and the lawyers of his day for doing just that. Jesus said directly *to* them, "You shut the door of the kingdom of heaven in people's faces." (Matthew 23:13)

Jesus said *of* them, "They bind together burdens heavy and grievous to be borne, and lay upon the shoulders of men, but with their finger they will not move them." (Matthew 23:4, YLT)

I never want to hear those words directed at me.

How Jesus Loved People

But woe to you, scribes and Pharisees, hypocrites! For you shut the kingdom of heaven in people's faces. For you neither enter yourselves nor allow those who would enter to go in.

The disciples were eating some food, and maybe they were feeling especially hungry because they dove in without washing first. Some Pharisees and lawyers gathered around and began to criticize Jesus for it: "What's with your disciples eating with defiled hands?" they asked. "Why don't they follow our tradition of washing before eating?"

Jesus takes this opportunity to explain to them the problem with their traditions. And he really lets them have it: "Isaiah was right when he prophesied about you hypocrites . . . You have a way of setting aside the commands of God and prioritizing your own traditions! For Moses said, 'Honor your father and mother . . .' But you say that if anyone declares what might have been used as Corban [that is, devoted to God] then you no longer let them give to their father or mother. So you nullify the word of God by your tradition . . . And you do many things like that." (Mark 7:1–13)

Now washing before eating is a good thing, but there are other more important priorities in God's way of thinking. Jesus said to them that their emphasis on washing and their other traditions were hindering people from entering into the kingdom of heaven.

When Jesus talks to them about their tradition of Corban, he's talking about their tradition of setting something apart and devoting it to God. Again, I think we can all agree that this is a good tradition. Setting something apart and dedicating it to God is commendable. The problem was that some of the Pharisees of Jesus' day took this to such an extreme that the dedicated thing was off-limits to use in any other fashion, even if it meant violating God's commandment to honor one's father or mother. They were so wrapped up in their traditions that when an elderly parent was in need, the Pharisees and lawyers wouldn't permit a person to help their own mom or dad.

Like Me, or Like Jesus

I've come to realize that I have great potential to open the door to the kingdom of heaven, or, to slam the door of the kingdom of heaven, and so do you. Whether or not that door is opened wide, or slammed in someone's face, depends on me, and depends on you. Like the Pharisees, our own traditions can shut the door of the kingdom of heaven on people. But Jesus loved people by opening up that door. Sometimes we lose sight of loving like Jesus because of *our* traditions. We become more concerned about conforming someone into our own image, than we do about conforming ourselves into the image of Jesus, and loving the way he does.

We can become focused on trying to make our wife, or our husband, or our son-in-law, or our friend, relative, or even our enemy, like us. We can focus on making our spouse clean up around the house the way we do. We can become upset when our son-in-law doesn't parent the way we would. We can focus on trying to make our friend's politics like our politics. We can focus on making our fellow Christian's theology like our theology. We can focus on making people like us. And other people can focus on making us like them.

But when we do, we focus amiss. Focusing on making people like ourselves is just a distraction from Jesus' commandment for us to love like Jesus. I think the reason so many of us fall into this pattern is that it's so much easier. It's so much easier for me to criticize or complain about the way in which someone else is not conformed into my own image politically, or theologically, or in the way they do things around the house, than it is for me to seek God's Holy Spirit's help in conforming me into the image of Jesus.

Instead of focusing on making other people like me, I need to focus on making me like Jesus.

In the context of politics, Bob Goff puts it this way: Don't worry about what's happening in the oval office, concern yourself with what's happening inside the oval around you. There are people inside that oval. Jesus commanded you to love them.[1]

So can I encourage you? If you're a Republican who has an established tradition of buying American, don't let the fact someone owns a Toyota Prius get in the way of you opening up God's kingdom to that person. If you're a Democrat who traditionally leaves a small carbon footprint, open the door wide to that guy who drives a Dodge Ram Mega Cab pickup.

Maybe the most common way in which we shut the door of God's kingdom on people occurs when we become distracted in this way. When the tradition of our worldview wins out over God's Spirit in our lives, we repel people away from the kingdom of heaven, we shut the door. Of course that's what this book is all about, opening the door of heaven to people by loving them like Jesus.

Our traditions. We can be very passionate about them. Flesh vs. Spirit, Republican vs. Democrat, Maddow vs. Hannity, Android vs. iPhone. Our traditions can be a closed door between heaven and the people around us.

Love Like Jesus

"You have a way of setting aside the commands of God in order to establish your own traditions!" Jesus said.

Let those words never be spoken to you or to me.

Let's never let our big opinions get in Jesus' way. Whatever your traditions, even though they're good traditions, don't let them shut the door of heaven on someone. Don't let them get in the way of Jesus' command to love.

Don't let them get in the way of loving like Jesus.

Notes:
1. Bob Goff, 10/1/2017 Teaching At Westside: A Jesus Church

2. 2
- Delany - Daily chemo -
  lung cancer
- Paul Lile - PT working
- Kelli - Feb. 13th - Appointment
- Alesha- Happy w/ new boyfriend
  - Toni daughter   'Casey'

(Jason Placeway - Chiropractor)

2-9
- Deb's hip pain
- Kelli - 13th - Mayfield
- Holly - colonoscopy
- Palmy - chemo - tumor shrank
- JT - tumor benign

CHAPTER 16

Love Like Jesus

Make Friends with Money

*. . . You cannot serve God and money. The
Pharisees, who were lovers of money, heard
all these things, and they ridiculed him.*
LUKE 16:13–14

How Jesus Loved People

The Pharisees ridiculed Jesus. Because Jesus had just made the
statement: "You cannot serve God and money."

And the Pharisees loved money.

So they ridiculed Jesus.

I've noticed many of us Christians have a tendency to tap dance
around the topic of greed. Maybe that's partly because of its subtlety.
We all need money to live, right? But how do you know when you've
stepped over the line? "When someone commits adultery," says Timothy

Keller, "they don't say, 'Oh, hey, wait a second, you're not my wife!'" But when we get greedy it's hard to recognize it. I think greed may be the most difficult sin to recognize in ourselves.[1]

When it comes to greed in the Bible, it might surprise you to know that, with few exceptions, God's heroes didn't struggle with it. Most of them struggled with other sins, but not greediness. And of course, Jesus never fell into any sin, including the sin of greed. Jesus seemed inclined to spend money on others.

Jesus loved people by giving, generously.

Jesus on Generosity: Make Friends with Money
To put the verse at the beginning of this chapter in context, Jesus, shortly before his statement, "You cannot serve God and money," told the parable about a manager who was guilty of mismanaging his rich master's possessions. Just before this guy was about to be fired, he called in his master's debtors and forgave a percentage of debt for each of them. He did it to change his future circumstances. He did it so he would be welcomed into their homes after he lost his job. (Luke 16:1–8)

In the very next verse, Jesus tells us to do the same. He says,

> *And I tell you, make friends for yourselves by means of unrighteous wealth, so that when it fails they may receive you into the eternal dwellings.*
> *Luke 16:9*

I used to think that manager who was about to get fired was a scoundrel. But now I recognize I have more in common with him than I like to think. I've come to realize there are at least three things we all have in common with that manager.

1. *The manager's resources aren't his own.*

In Jesus' parable all the resources belong to the master. It's the same for me, and it's the same for you. When I'm doing well I like to give myself the credit. But in reality, everything I have was given to me by God. Every good and perfect gift comes from above. (James 1:17) I have some material blessings, and I say it was *my* hard work and *my* brains and *my* energy that brought in those blessings. But who gave me my brains? And who gave me the drive to work hard? And who gave me all that energy? The answer is that it all came from above, it all came from God, it all came from my Master. I like to think of it as my own but it's not. Everything I have is my Master's. Every breath I breathe comes from Him. (Genesis 2:7)

2. *The manager is guilty of mismanagement.*

The manager in Jesus' parable was guilty of mismanaging his master's resources, and so am I, every single time I sin. And so are you every time you sin. And so are we all. We all sin. None are righteous. Jesus leveled the playing field in his sermon on the mount. Every single one of us is guilty of sin. Every single one of us is guilty of mismanaging our Master's resources. Cain mismanaged the strength God gave him when he murdered his brother Abel. David mismanaged the leisure time, the celebrity, and the vitality God gave him when he sinned with Bathsheba. Aaron mismanaged the resources of the Israelites when he crafted the gold idol. Whenever we sin we're mismanaging in some way. You could even say when we sin we're mismanaging the very life God blessed us with.

3. *The manager had opportunity to change his future.*

The manager who was guilty of mismanagement had the opportunity to change his future life. He could have been passive. He could have just taken his pink slip and entered into a life on the street. But he didn't. He took initiative and was generous with his master's resources so that he would be welcomed into dwellings after his life of employment was over. I have the same opportunity. I also can choose to be generous with my Master's resources to impact my future. In verse nine, when Jesus says to us, ". . . I tell you, make friends for yourselves by means of unrighteous wealth, so that when it fails they may receive you into the eternal dwellings," Jesus is telling us to take the opportunity to be generous with the resources God has given us.

So no, you can't take material wealth with you when you die, but apparently, according to Jesus, you can send it ahead.

According to Tim Keller, following this teaching of Jesus to make friends with generosity in this way is one of the reasons the early church grew so rapidly. There's an ancient letter from a man named Diognetus, and in it he says the reason the church grew so fast is because, "we share our table with all, but we do not share our bed with all." In other words, during that time, in that culture, the early Christ followers were generous with their material possessions, and kept their bodies for their spouses. This was in contrast to the unbelievers of that time who were stingy with their money, but promiscuous with their bodies.[1]

How to Love Like Jesus

John, a former skeptic and current Christ follower from our church, once found out about a single woman who had a serious health problem.

John's wife Jenny worked with her at Starbucks and noticed she was experiencing weakness and dizziness. Throughout the workday she would have to stop and take a minute to sit down to recover. John and his wife also found out that this woman had taken on a second job. In spite of her weakened condition, she had no choice. She was in debt because the necessary treatment was expensive. Her medical bills were mounting.

So John and Jenny met with her after work one day, and they gave her a significant sum of money. And they said to her, "We want to give this to you, because we know that Jesus loves us, and Jesus loves you too. And we know that you're going through this, that you're suffering. So this is relief. There's no strings attached. Spend it on whatever you want. Spend it on medical bills, spend it on groceries, we're not going to track it. It's yours."

She was surprised. She sat there and didn't say anything for a long while, and then, at a certain point, she said, "You guys know I'm gay, right?"

And they did know. And they told her they knew. And they told her that all they wanted to do was to show her that love. The love of Jesus.

This woman was blown away because the only image of a Christian she had was a caricature she carried around inside her mind. And that caricature carried a bullhorn and screamed at people it disagreed with.[3]

John and Jenny's gift was unexpected, and the amount was enough to surprise the woman in need. And that's how we see Jesus love people. When you're in a crowd of thousands in a remote location and Jesus feeds everybody, you're surprised. When you've been blind from birth and Jesus gives you vision, it's astounding. When Jesus helped someone, their expectations were almost always exceeded. His help was unexpected and surprising, "like an unforeseen kiss" as David Crowder puts it in his song "How He Loves."

My observation has been that people who love like Jesus by giving, tend to give the way John and Jenny gave, in a way that's unexpected and surprising.

I knew a twenty-something named Greg who died young. While he was alive he liked to walk around downtown Portland and ask homeless people how he could help them. Then he'd deliver to them a sleeping bag, or a meal, or some other basic necessity. I know a man named Robert who does something similar in a town near me. He just walks around downtown, praying, and looking for people he can help. And sometimes that help is in the form of giving materially. When these men help people, they often do it in a way that's surprising and exceeds the expectations of the receiver.

Inspired by Jesus and these examples of people who love like Jesus, Kathy and I set up a bank account with a debit card. The sole purpose of that account is to help people who can't pay us back (as Jesus described when he said to help those who can't pay back in Luke 14:12–14). Sometimes we'll walk around prayerfully hoping to encounter people who need help, and then we use the money from that account to help them. More often we just encounter someone who needs help during the course of our normal day's activities. I ask myself sometimes: What would the world look like if all Christ followers did this? Would we experience rapid growth similar to the time of Diognetus? It's so easy to fall into the trap of studying how to love like Jesus, but never actually engaging in the act of loving people. Love is a verb. Love does, as Bob Goff would say.[2] The manager took the initiative when he used his master's resources to help people with their debts. Jesus tells us to do the same. Loving like Jesus involves active generosity.

I'm not discounting the more common ways of giving. Tithing, giving extra to your church, giving to missions are all great ways to give. I'm just saying Jesus tended to give in a way that was surprising and exceeded expectations. That's how he loved people.

Jesus Wasn't Much of a Dancer

At the beginning of this chapter, I wrote that we tap dance around the issue of greed because of its subtlety. But there's another reason. The main reason I think many of us dance around this issue is for the same reason the Pharisees ridiculed Jesus—we simply love money. And we've become very clever about justifying our love for it. We're skilled at rationalizing why we don't turn loose of our money (which is really God's money) to help those who can't pay us back.

But Jesus spoke plainly and directly on this issue: The love of money is bad, and generosity is good. (Luke 16:1–17, 19–31, see also 1 Timothy 6:10.)

The Pharisees dismissed Jesus' teachings about serving God and not money. I want to encourage you to run in the opposite direction of those Pharisees. To love like Jesus, make your heavenly Father the ultimate in your life. Seek God's kingdom first. Use the money your Master has blessed you with to show Jesus' love to others. Give in a way that's surprising and exceeds expectations. (Matthew 6:33)

That's how Jesus loved people.

That's how you can love like Jesus.

No servant can serve two masters, for either he will hate the one and love the other, or he will be devoted to the one and despise the other. You cannot serve God and money.
Luke 16:13

87

Notes:
1. Timothy Keller Teaching, "Preaching Today" Tape #230, May 2, 1999, via Christianity Today, URL: http://www.preachingtoday.com/sermons/sermons/2005/august/230.html
2. Bob Goff, *Love Does,* Thomas Nelson, 2012
3. Marcus Davis, "Seeing Jesus," Colossae Church, April 8, 2018, URL: http://tigard.colossaechurch.org/messages/

Part Two

Practical Help

CHAPTER 17

Love Like Jesus

Jesus and the 5 Love Languages

. . . just as I have loved you, you also are to love one another.
JOHN 13:34

How I Removed "I Love You" from My Vocabulary

While I was researching this book, I was thinking about how Jesus is never quoted as saying the words "I love you."

So toward my goal to love people the way Jesus loved people, I decided to try it. I decided to try it for about a week. So for about one week, I took the phrase "I love you," out of my vocabulary.

And what happened? It turns out that removing "I love you" from my vocabulary was one of the most powerful practices I've ever implemented.

As a writer who works at home, most of my time is spent with my wife Kathy. And I love her. I mean I'm crazy about her. But that week

I was under this self-imposed vow of silence when it came to saying the words "I love you." So what happened was this pressure very quickly built, until I was almost bursting inside to find ways to express my love for Kathy. Not saying "I love you," was like putting a cork in the bottle of bubbling emotion inside of my body. Suddenly I just had to find a way, a way to communicate to my wife how much I loved her.

So I acted. I acted because—what else could I do, but act? I expressed my love through acts of service. Nothing major, just small gestures during the course of the week. I cleaned the kitchen. I cleaned the garage. I did some yard work. And I expressed my love through a gift, again nothing spectacular, just a small gift. I bought Kathy some flowers. And the result was, in my quest to love like Jesus, that was one of the best weeks of my life. Who knew not saying those particular words could have such a powerful effect?

I want to encourage you to try it sometime. Take the words "I love you," out of your vocabulary for a week and find creative ways to express your love for people. Try it, especially if you're like me and you tend to communicate love using words.

Try it and see what happens.

It will help you to love like Jesus.

Jesus and the 5 Love Languages

In Gary Chapman's classic book, *The 5 Love Languages*, he identifies five distinct ways in which love is communicated. According to Chapman, the five emotional love languages are: "Words of Affirmation," "Quality Time," "Receiving Gifts," "Acts of Service," and "Physical Touch." The premise of the book is that problems arise when one person's love language doesn't match up with another's, but relationships can flourish when you communicate with someone using their primary love language.

In my and Kathy's example above, we see Chapman's principles at work. I'm a person whose primary love language is the language of "Affirming Words." As Mark Twain famously said, "I can live for two months on a good compliment." That's me. But Kathy's primary love language is the language of "Acts of Service." It's instinctive for me to show my love for Kathy with "Words of Affirmation" because that's my personal primary love language. It's natural for me to offer compliments, words of encouragement, and words of appreciation. It feels right for me to say "I love you." But I can offer up words of affirmation for days on end without eliciting much of a response from Kathy. What Kathy responds to is when I do the dishes, or install the natural gas hookup for the barbecue, or help her paint the outside of the house. She loves it when I say "I love you" by doing. I love it when she says "I love you" by telling.

And then there's Jesus. In the course of my study of Jesus, I couldn't help but notice that he used all five love languages throughout his time on earth.

1. Acts of Service: Jesus' First Love Language

One of the most famous acts of service performed by Jesus occurred the night before his crucifixion. Jesus rose from supper, his last supper, laid aside his outer garments, and wrapped a towel around his waist. Then he poured water into a basin and washed his disciples' feet, wiping them with the towel. He went on to speak to his disciples about the importance of loving people through service.

After he finished washing his disciples' feet, he put his outer garments back on and returned to his place at the table. And he said,

Do you understand what I have done to you? You call me Teacher and Lord, and rightly so, because I am. So if I then, your

Lord and Teacher, have washed your feet, you also ought to wash
one another's feet. For I've given you an example, that you should
do just as I have done to you.
   . . . If you know these things, blessed are you if you do them.
John 13:1–15, 17

My career as a firefighter was filled with rescuing, and attempts at rescuing, people from death, illness, injury, and other problems. And people call that vocation the fire *service*. As firefighters, when we rescued someone we served them. And anytime Jesus rescued someone from death, illness, injury, or any other problem, he communicated God's love with an act of service.

While Jesus was traveling to Jairus' house where Jairus' twelve-year-old daughter lay dying, a woman touched his garment. This woman who touched him had for years lived with a chronic discharge of blood. When she touched his garment she was healed immediately.

And at the moment she was healed, Jesus said, "Who touched me?"

The way the large crowd was "pressing in on" him made the disciples question why he would ask such a question.

But Jesus said, "Someone touched me, for I perceive that power has gone out of me." (Luke 8:44–46)

I see this as an indication that every time Jesus healed someone, power went out from him. That's how it is with an act of service. Power goes out from you and power goes out from me every time we perform an act of service. And usually it's power in the form of our physical or emotional energy.

Jesus spit on the ground and made mud, then he anointed the blind man's eyes with the mud and the man could see. Jesus put his fingers into the deaf man's ears and said to him, "Ephphatha," (be opened) and his ears were opened. Jesus led another blind man by the hand, out of the village, he spit on his eyes and lay hands on him, twice, and the man could see. There are thirty-one individual healings of Jesus recorded in the Bible, and additionally, there are eleven times when the Bible records that Jesus healed many. And each required power to go out from Jesus. And each is an example of how Jesus loved through an act of service. (John 9:6–7, Mark 7:32–35, Mark 8:23–26)

Do This, and You'll Be Blessed

"For I have given you an example," Jesus said, "that you also should do just as I have done to you." Craig Keener, one of my favorite Bible commentators, says of this verse, "Disciples were to learn especially by imitating their teachers." That's the point of this book, to persuade you to do everything you can to imitate Jesus, and in so doing, to love like Jesus. (John 13:15)

When it comes to imitating Jesus through serving, it will take your energy and time. Power will go out of you, but it will be worth it. Because a few verses after his call for us to imitate his example, Jesus says to us, "If you know these things, blessed are you if you do them."

If we imitate Jesus' behavior in this passage, if we "through love serve one another," we'll not only bless others, but we'll be blessed. I know the most fulfilling times in my life have been those times when I served others. Serving myself has always left me feeling empty. (Galatians 5:13)

The Ultimate Act of Service

Jesus washing his disciples' feet not only gives us an example to follow on a practical level, but he provides a physical picture of what he did on a cosmic level too.

Jesus interrupts his supper to remove his outer garment even as Jesus interrupted his time at his Father's throne in heaven to remove his glory. (Philippians 2:7–8)

Jesus wraps himself in a towel even as he wrapped himself in the flesh when he took the form of a human being here on earth.

Jesus humbled himself when he washed the disciples' feet, even as he humbled himself when he came to earth to serve. Jesus himself said,

> *For even the Son of Man came not to be served but to serve,*
> *and to give his life as a ransom for many.*
> *Mark 10:45*

Earlier in this chapter, I mentioned that Jesus served whenever he rescued someone from death. Jesus did that when he raised Lazarus, Jairus' daughter, and the son of a widow from the dead, physically. But Jesus' ultimate act of service, his ultimate rescue, came when he took the weight of the sins of the world upon himself, when he sacrificed himself in your place, and in my place, so we could be saved from our sins.

Jesus' ultimate act of service came at the expense of his life.

When he laid it down for you and for me.

2. Words of Affirmation

Jesus said of John the Baptist that he is "more than a prophet" and "among those born of women there has arisen no one greater." These are some of the most powerful words of affirmation recorded in the entire Bible. They're powerful because of the words themselves, and they're also powerful because they're indirect words of affirmation. Chapman writes that words spoken to *others* about a person are more powerful, because when the person who is the object of the words finds out indirectly, he or she knows the words weren't meant for any other purpose than to affirm. (Matthew 11:9–11)

When Jesus heard that the centurion believed Jesus could heal his servant with a word, right from where Jesus was geographically, without being physically present with the sick servant, Jesus commended him publicly. He said, "I tell you, not even in Israel have I found such faith." (See Luke 7:1–10.)

In Matthew 12:49 Jesus stretches out his hand toward his disciples and tells the crowd that they are his family.

In the book of Mark, when the woman anointed Jesus with oil from her alabaster flask, Jesus told the crowd at the dinner party, "She has done a beautiful thing," and "wherever the gospel is proclaimed in the whole world, what she has done will be told in memory of her." (Mark 14:6–9)

And Jesus affirmed Peter when Peter identifies Jesus as "the Christ, the Son of the living God." (Matthew 16:15–17)

(See also Mark 12:34, and Mark 12:43.)

3. Quality Time

To you has been given the secret of the kingdom of God, but for those outside everything is in parables . . .

Jesus lived with his disciples for three years. For three years they were together. They worked together, shared sleeping quarters together, ate together. And they enjoyed quality time apart from the crowds. It was during such a time that Jesus, alone with his disciples, privately shared the meaning of the parable of the sower of the seed. These occasions of quality time alone with his disciples occurred regularly. ". . . Privately to his own disciples he explained everything." (Mark 4:10–11, Mark 4:34)

One time, when Jesus and his disciples were passing through Galilee, Jesus "did not want anyone to know, for he was teaching his disciples" about his death and resurrection. So we see that Jesus guarded his quality time with those closest to him. (Mark 9:30–31)

Another time "Jesus took with him Peter and James, and John his brother, and led them up a high mountain by themselves." When Jesus was transfigured on that mountain top, the time was shared with only three of his disciples. (Matthew 17:1–9)

Not long before he would be taken away by the authorities and killed, Jesus gathered his disciples and they ate, talked, took the first communion, sung a hymn, and prayed. In the book of John, we see that Jesus also washed the feet of his disciples during this time. In fact, in the book of John, five chapters are devoted to the documentation of the quality time Jesus invested in his disciples before his crucifixion. (Matthew 26:20–39, John chapters 13–17)

But Jesus didn't just spend time with his disciples. He reclined at table with tax collectors and sinners too, and the Pharisees complained about the quality time Jesus spent with such a crowd. (Luke 5:29–30)

(See also Matthew 15:12–20, Matthew 20:17, Mark 2:15.)

4. Giving Gifts

The night of the last supper, Jesus said to Judas, "What you are going to do, do quickly." Because Judas had the money bag, when Jesus said those words the disciples thought Jesus might have told him to "give something to the poor." The disciples' assumption makes it obvious that Jesus was in the habit of giving gifts. (John 13:27–29)

Jesus gave the four thousand the gift of food to eat in Matthew chapter 15.

Jesus gave the five thousand the gift of bread and fish in Luke chapter 9.

Before Jesus sent out his twelve disciples, he gave them the gift of power and authority to cure diseases and to cast out demons. (Luke 9:1)

"When you give to the needy, sound no trumpet before you," Jesus said.

"*When* you give to the needy."

Jesus said, "when," not "if." (Matthew 6:2)

Jesus was a giver of gifts.

(See also Mark 10:17–27.)

5. Physical Touch

When the children came to Jesus we see that "he took them in his arms and blessed them, laying hands on them." (Mark 10:15–16)

In Matthew 17:7 we read, "Jesus came and touched them, saying, "Rise, and have no fear."

In Matthew 18:14–15 we read, "He touched her hand and the fever left her."

When Jesus saw Simon's mother-in-law lying ill, he "took her by the hand and lifted her up, and the fever left her." (Mark 1:31)

"Those who had any who were sick with various diseases brought them to him, and *he laid his hands on every one of them* and healed them." (Luke 4:40, emphasis mine)

Jesus didn't have to touch. As the centurion pointed out in Luke 7, Jesus is perfectly capable of healing with a word from a remote location. But he usually didn't do it that way. He usually chose to be physically present.

And he made it a point to physically touch.

How to Love Like Jesus

Noticing what kind of love language different people are receptive to is essential to loving like Jesus. In the context of a marriage relationship,

Chapman writes: "Your emotional love language and the language of your spouse may be as different as Chinese from English. No matter how hard you try to express love in English, if your spouse understands only Chinese, you will never understand how to love each other."

The week I didn't say "I love you" to Kathy was successful for two reasons. The first was because I imitated Jesus. The second was because I was speaking Kathy's primary love language, "Acts of Service."

The 5 Love Languages was first published in 1995. Every year since it has sold more than the year before. Walk into any brick-and-mortar bookstore and you'll find it on the bestseller shelf. It's been on that shelf for years. I believe the reason it's so successful, and the reason it works, is because Chapman captured five ways Jesus loved people.

Chapman writes that the communication of love isn't without nuance. There are many "dialects" of love within the five. His five love languages are the five *basic* languages of love.

But the point is, if you're trying to communicate the love of Jesus to someone in the wrong love language, your chances for success are diminished considerably.

In the context of loving like Jesus:

> *Your emotional love language and the language of the person you're trying to love like Jesus may be as different as Chinese from English. No matter how hard you try to express love in English, if the other person understands only Chinese, you will never understand how to love that person.[1]*

Jesus used all five love languages, and undoubtedly he was a master at matching them with people appropriately. But even Jesus identified people's love languages by listening. "What do you want me to do for you?" he asked the blind man in Luke 18:41.

He also identified how to communicate love effectively, simply by identifying a serious problem. If someone is obviously destitute, "Receiving Gifts" will likely be an effective love language. If someone is sick or injured, you can anticipate that "Acts of Service" that move that person toward healing will be an effective way to communicate love. The greater the person's urgent need, the easier it is to identify the person's love language. You've noticed by now who Jesus primarily chose to minister to: the blind, the lame, the lepers, the poor. He liked to love people with problems. And he communicated his love by solving those problems. An urgent need is a shortcut to understanding a person's love language.

So to love like Jesus, be mindful of the different ways different people receive love. Listen to the people around you to learn their love languages. And find people with problems whose love languages are easily identifiable.

Recognize that communicating Jesus' love in the appropriate language is an important part of loving like Jesus.

Notes
Further study will be rewarded. I highly recommend the book *The 5 Love Languages*.

1. Gary Chapman, *The 5 Love Languages: The Secret to Love That Lasts*, Northfield Publishing, 2014

2-23

Brake- bach, rest, Amelie's weight

Oliver- 27th - sugary

CHAPTER 18

Love Like Jesus

Jesus and Anger

The Chapter about Anger that Might Make You Angry

I have to confess, I was reluctant to include this chapter about anger, because I'm concerned it will make people angry. But, maybe, in spite of my better judgment . . .

Jesus Nerd

If you follow my Instagram, Twitter, or other social media accounts you know I frequently post scripture. More than one person has criticized me for it, but what can I say—I'm a Jesus nerd. I've become fascinated by this ancient Jewish Rabbi, so much so that I just can't help myself; I want to learn as much as I can about him, and I want to share him with others. One time I posted the words from Jesus,

". . . I say to you that everyone who is angry with his brother will be liable to judgment . . ." (Matthew 5:22) And a friend of mine, Jimmy, asked in the comment section, "What do you think is meant by 'brother'?"

Now some friends ask questions I can answer off the top of my head, and other friends ask questions that require digging around in the scriptures. Jimmy's questions tend to fall into the latter category, so, I dug around in the scriptures to see what the Bible says about it. And what I found probably isn't what you'd expect.

Who Is My Brother?

The easy part of the answer is addressing the specific question, "Who is my brother?" I think when you heard this question, you might have had another scripture come to mind. The one where the expert in the law asks Jesus, "Who is my neighbor?"

Jesus responded with a parable that made clear the emphasis of the scripture in question, "Love your neighbor as yourself," was about love, and not identifying who's a neighbor and who's not a neighbor. I think in the same way, Jesus' words, "everyone who is angry with his brother will be liable to judgment" might be about the anger we sometimes find in our hearts, rather than identifying who's our brother and who's not. (Luke 10:25-37)

Jesus' statement about anger is part of his great Sermon on the Mount, where he also says, ". . . whoever insults his brother will be liable to the council; and whoever says, 'You fool!' will be liable to the hell of fire."

And, ". . . everyone who looks at a woman with lustful intent has already committed adultery with her in his heart." (Matthew chapter 5)

In the Sermon on the Mount, Jesus is saying: It's not just your outward action, but the real issue is in your heart, the inner workings of your soul and your mind. It's not just the act of adultery, but it's the lust inside of you. It's not just the act of murder, but it's the anger inside of you. And of course every one of us feels lust, and every one of us feels anger. So Jesus makes us all equally guilty. He levels the playing field.

None is righteous, no not one. (Romans 3:10)

We're all sinners.

We're all dependent on God's grace. We're all dependent on Jesus and his sacrifice on the cross, on our behalf. We're all sinners, and one of the sins common to us all is anger. We all get angry.

The Surprising Part

Most of my life I heard Bible teachers—Bible teachers I love, and appreciate, and respect—teach me to "Be angry and sin not . . ." That's from Ephesians chapter 4, verse 26 (KJV). They said, "Paul tells us to 'be angry,' so we can be sure that anger's not a sin. It's what we do with anger that can be sinful." And they pointed out that God expresses anger in the Old Testament. And they told me that Jesus became angry when the Pharisees didn't want him to heal on the Sabbath, and when he drove out the money changers.

I really liked that, because it gave me permission to be angry. If I saw some injustice, or something I disagreed with, or some innocent person who was hurt by another, I could crank up the righteous anger. And it felt good when I did.

But then one day I became angry with Kathy. (It was the very next day after one of the best weeks of my life loving like Jesus that I wrote about in the "5 Love Languages" chapter.) The day I became angry I threw a plate in the sink, and, I slammed the front door of our house on my fingers as I stormed out. So there I was, standing outside our front door, I could already see the color of my throbbing fingers changing to black and blue. I desperately needed ice and ibuprofen, but I was too proud to go back in. So I drove around aimlessly until the pain finally grew to the point where it was greater than my pride—about fifteen minutes. On my way back, less than a mile from the house on NW 185th Avenue, I turned on the local Christian radio station hoping for inspiration. And the first words out of the speakers were, "The anger of man does not produce the righteousness of God." (James 1:20)

Those words were from an interview with Brant Hansen, the author of the book *Unoffendable*. Given the circumstances, I thought it might be a good idea to read that book, so I did. That book, and more importantly, researching what the Bible has to say about anger, has made me realize something: The Bible doesn't say about anger what I thought the Bible said about anger.[1]

"Be angry and sin not," is certainly there, in the Bible, in black and white, along with a few other verses that tell us to be "slow to anger." But every one of the Bible teachers who leaned on those few verses when they taught about anger, also taught that we should never take verses out of context, but we should consider the whole counsel of God. Most Christ-followers know that to be true. And I can't remember a single time when any of those Bible teachers ever did take a single verse or just a few verses here and there out of context.

Except when it came to anger.

Because just a little farther down the page from "Be angry and sin not," we see in the same chapter of Ephesians, "Let all bitterness and wrath and anger and clamor and slander be put away from you, along with all malice." (Ephesians 4:31)

Let "all" anger be put away from you, we're instructed. This is the kind of place where my favorite Bible teachers usually say, "And 'all' in the Greek means: 'all'." Except when it comes to anger—they don't.

Also, consider this: In the wisdom literature of the Bible (Job, Psalms, Proverbs, Song of Solomon, Ecclesiastes), anger is almost always associated with a fool or foolishness.

In Colossians 3:8 we're instructed again: "You must put them all away: anger, wrath, malice, slander, and obscene talk from your mouth." (There's that word "all" again.)

Psalm 37:8 says, "Refrain from anger, and forsake wrath! Fret not yourself; it tends only to evil."

And then there's the scripture in James, ". . . the anger of man does not produce the righteousness of God."

And then there are Jesus' words from the Sermon on the Mount. And there's more besides.

It's overwhelming. When you really dig around and see what the Bible says, as a whole, not just a few verses, but as a whole, it's overwhelming. I don't think I ever saw this until recently because I didn't want to see it. When it comes to what the Bible teaches about anger, I like that one verse, Ephesians 4:26: "Be angry and do not sin . . ." And I like it all by itself. Because when it comes to what the Bible teaches about anger, my perspective requires that I take this verse in isolation.

To justify my personal anger, it's necessary to take Ephesians 4:26 by itself, out of context. The part that comes later in the same chapter that says, let all anger be put away from you, I want to edit. I want to interject a little phrase into that verse that says, "except for righteous anger." That's the phrase I want to add to the other places in the Bible that talk about anger too. That's how I operate. I love the parts of the Bible I agree with, but there are a lot of places where I'd like to add a little phrase, or include a little qualifying statement, so I can fit the Bible into the framework of my own personal preferences and worldview, and make it match my current patterns of thought and behavior.

But What About God and Jesus' Anger?

Some Bible teachers have said that we can (and even should) be angry because God and Jesus were angry. But the reality is, some things that are permissible or allowable or even good and desirable for God and Jesus, aren't good and desirable for us.

Vengeance is like that. We love a movie like *Taken* with Liam Neeson. "I don't have money, but what I do have are a very particular set of skills . . . Skills that make me a nightmare for people like you. If you let my daughter go now, that'll be the end of it."

But of course, the bad guys didn't let his daughter go. And it felt so good to watch Liam Neeson have his vengeance. But the Bible doesn't provide for our own personal vengeance. "Vengeance is mine, I will repay, says the Lord." (Romans 12:19)

And judgment is like that too. Judgment belongs to God. Because for us, judging others only results in judgment against ourselves. (Matthew 7:1-5) Jesus Christ is the one appointed by God as Judge, and I'm glad for that. It's amazingly freeing when you realize, God wants Jesus to judge, and He commands us to love. I'm thankful for that. I want God to have the position of Judge because His judgment is perfect. If I were judge, my human frailties and limitations would surely make a mess of things. (John 5:27, Acts 10:42)

Anger is in the same category as vengeance and judgment. It makes sense because of His perfection. My anger is imperfect and never produces the righteousness of God. My anger can be capricious, self-indulgent, irritable, and morally ignoble. But His anger is appropriate because He is perfectly just and incapable of making a mistake. (Packer)[2]

Why Would God Want To Withhold Anger From Us?

Like everything else God wants to withhold from us, He wants us to put away all anger because it's destructive. It's destructive to the one who becomes angry. The Amplified Bible says in Proverbs 14:30 that "A calm and undisturbed mind and heart are the life and health of the body, but envy, jealousy, and wrath are like rottenness of the bones." How true that is. According to the Cleveland Clinic, a big focus of heart disease research used to be on type A personalities. But now researchers have determined that "it's the specific characteristic of anger—or hostility—that stresses the heart and leads to an eventual cardiac event." Men who are quick to anger are more likely to develop premature heart disease and five times more likely to have an early heart attack.

Anger causes a cortisol dump into your system. Anger alters the balance in the nervous system of your heart. Anger increases inflammatory markers. Anger kills.[3]

And it doesn't just kill the person carrying the anger.

Anger kills relationships too.

Anger kills love.

Love Gone Wrong

I've heard it said that an emotion is not a sin. But I've also heard it said that emotions gone wrong are sin. That's easy to see with love and lust. Lust for another outside of your marriage is love gone wrong. It's a twist on the emotion of love, and it's a sin. (Matthew 5:27-30) Anger, strangely, is also the emotion of love gone wrong. All you have to do to see that, is ask yourself what you're defending the next time you feel angry. When I'm running late, I get angry at bad drivers in traffic. But what I'm defending is how I'll look to the people who expect me to be on time. I'm angry because I *love* to look good to others.

I once heard a wise man define anger with these two words: "Violated expectations." When I expect someone to behave a certain way, and they don't meet my expectations, I become angry. The Pharisees expected Jesus to not mess with their religious hierarchy and to fall in line with their religious customs, but Jesus didn't meet their expectations, and they became angry. So they killed him.

They became angry because Jesus was a threat to what they loved: their position of power in Jewish society and the traditions of men in their religious system.

I'm afraid we find ourselves in precisely the same place as the Pharisees. There's power in anger, and when we're angry, we're afforded a position of power. Our tradition is our established patterns of thinking and behaving. What Jesus said in the Sermon on the Mount, and what God tells us to do with anger throughout the whole of scripture, threaten them both.

You Know You'll Get Angry So, Plan For It

I know for certain that at some point in the future I'm going to become angry. That's true for all of us. And our response will be dramatically improved if we already have a plan in place for how we'll handle it.

If you're calm enough, I think the best response is to ask yourself, "What can I say and do that would most please God right now?" And then do that. Tony Dungy, the Super Bowl winning football coach, has a similar strategy. When he feels anger rising, he asks himself, "What can I do to most help the situation?"[4]

Another suggestion comes from Dr. Joe Martin. His pre-planned response to feelings of anger is to first identify what he's afraid of, because all anger is rooted in fear this helps him to take the focus off the person he might be angry with. Then he recites a prayer that takes his focus off his expectations and puts his focus on God and what God wants.[5]

But sometimes, if we're flooded with emotion, we might not have the ability to say and do what pleases God the most. In those situations, if you feel anger rising, the best response is to leave as early in the chain of interaction as possible. Excuse yourself and go for a walk and pray. Or go hit the gym, or the driving range, or the basketball court. Or mow the lawn, or clean the house, or rake the leaves, or pound nails on your project. It's not healthy to let things fester, so you must find some form of release that doesn't hurt anybody or cause you to sin. Later when you and whoever you're communicating with are calm, you can revisit the issue.

So leave, and leave early in the interaction, before you feel flooded with emotion, pray at the earliest opportunity, find some form of release, and then revisit the issue later that day, or even the next day, when the conversation can be more constructive.

You can also be proactive about your anger. If you're feeling stressed, or if you know you're going to spend time with a certain someone who has a knack for getting under your skin, then hit the gym or engage in some other form of release a few hours before you're around that person. I have found this preemptive strike against anger to be a very effective tactic.

How To Love Like Jesus

Whatever your pre-planned response looks like, it's important to have one, because:

Anger kills relationships.

Anger kills love.

Anger can kill your ability to love like Jesus.

To love like Jesus, put away all anger.

> *"You must put them all away: anger, wrath, malice, slander, and obscene talk from your mouth." (Colossians 3:8)*

The Problem of Not Knowing

In Acts chapter 9 we learn something about our human limitations.

> *Now there was a disciple at Damascus named Ananias. The Lord said to him in a vision, "Ananias." And he said, "Here I am, Lord." And the Lord said to him, "Rise and go to the street called Straight, and at the house of Judas look for a man of Tarsus named Saul, for behold, he is praying, and he has seen in a vision a man named Ananias come in and lay his hands on him so that he might regain his sight." But Ananias answered, "Lord, I have heard from many about this man, how much evil he has done to your saints at Jerusalem. And here he has authority from the chief priests to bind all who call on your name." But the Lord said to him, "Go, for he is a chosen instrument of mine to carry my name before the Gentiles and kings and the children of Israel. For I will show him how much he must suffer for the sake of my name." So Ananias departed and entered the house. And laying his hands on him he said, "Brother Saul, the Lord Jesus who appeared to you on the road by which you came has sent me so that you may regain your sight and be filled with the Holy Spirit." And immediately something like scales fell from his eyes, and he regained his sight. Then he rose and was baptized; and taking food, he was strengthened.*
> *Acts 9:10-19*

I read this passage recently and I was struck by what Ananias didn't know. And that led me to think about the limitations of our knowledge as human beings and how we sometimes think we know things. And sometimes, the things we think we know cause us to rev up our righteous anger.

We Think We Know Things About Mothers Who Don't Take Care of Their Children

Michael was a Seventh-day Adventist pastor, Lindy was a pastor's wife, and Azaria was the name of their two-month-old daughter. They were camping in the Australian Outback when witnesses say they saw Lindy outside of her tent yelling, "A dingo's got my baby!"

According to *TIME* magazine, at the time, in Australia, there was speculation that followers of the Seventh-day Adventist religion sometimes sacrificed their babies. People even said the baby's name, Azaria, meant "sacrifice in the wilderness." And then there was the prevailing public opinion concerning dingoes. It was believed that a dingo would never attack a human being unprovoked. After the baby's disappearance, the public was sympathetic–toward the dingoes. Michael and Lindy were stoic in their grief which further fueled speculation that, since the dingoes couldn't possibly have done it, the couple must have killed their own daughter. They were charged, and convicted, of murder. The prosecution proposed that Lindy slit her daughter's throat with scissors, hid the body in a camera case, drove to a remote location away from their camp, and buried their deceased baby.

There was a media frenzy and the case received worldwide attention. They even made a movie about it starring Meryl Streep. The dog-like dingoes were facing a harsh accusation from Lindy and Michael. And the media, the public, and the prosecution all sided with the dingoes. During the trial, journalists published images of dingoes looking more playful than predatory. Lindy was convicted of murder and sentenced to life in prison. Her husband Michael was convicted of accessory after the fact. Lindy spent four years behind bars and away from her husband and her other three children. The couple eventually divorced. (Divorce rates increase as a result of imprisonment.)

People thought the idea that a dingo would crawl into a tent and drag away someone's baby was ludicrous–and they thought it was funny too. "A dingo's got my baby" evolved into "a dingo ate my baby." That phrase, spoken in an exaggerated Australian accent, became a favorite punchline of comedians. It appeared on popular sitcoms like *Seinfeld* and *The Simpsons*.

But the people, the prosecution, and the media were making a judgment without all the facts. Four years later more light was shed on the case: Azaria's clothes were found partially buried near a dingo lair. Before Azaria's death, the chief park ranger warned that the increasing dingo population in the area was becoming a danger to humans, but his warnings were ignored. It was also discovered that "blood stains" on the floor of Michael and Lindy's car were stains from a spilled drink. Since Lindy and Michael lost their daughter Azaria, three other small children have been attacked and killed by dingoes. Eventually, with all the facts in hand, the coroner came forward with a declaration that dingoes were responsible for the death of two-month-old Azaria. Lindy and Michael's names were cleared, but it took years. In the interim Lindy served time in prison and the family was torn apart. The real meaning of the name Azaria is "blessed of God," not sacrificed in the wilderness.[6]

We Think We Know Things About People Who Sue Other People

I remember hearing about the lady who bought coffee from McDonald's and spilled it on her lap. Then she sued and was awarded millions of dollars. That made a large group of people angry. And I was a part of that group. I mean, come on, give me a break. Coffee is supposed to be hot. It's not McDonald's fault she's grabbing coffee in the drive through and tries to open it while she's behind the wheel. She's just an idiot trying to game the system. Trying to get into McDonald's deep pockets. Where's the personal accountability here? I thought this way up until very recently as a matter of fact.

The other day I stumbled upon the facts about the case. The lady was 79-year-old Stella Liebeck. She wasn't even driving, she was a passenger. The car wasn't moving, it was parked after they left the drive thru. She suffered third degree burns that required skin grafts. She was just doing the best she could to get the lid off the coffee cup to add cream and sugar when it spilled on her lap. Stella was burned so badly that her genitalia fused to her inner thighs. And, it wasn't an isolated incident. McDonald's had received over 700 reports of injury from it's hot coffee including some others with third degree burns. In spite of all those reports McDonald's maintained its policy to serve their coffee hot—too hot. McDonald's continued to serve coffee at temperatures that cause third degree burns in three to seven seconds. Also, Stella offered to settle with McDonald's for $20k, just enough to cover her medical expenses, but McDonald's best offer was for only $800. During the trial the executives at McDonald's maintained an attitude that only 700 people burned was no big deal. I thought I knew who Stella Liebeck was and I was angry about how she sued McDonald's. I thought I knew things. But I really didn't.[7]

We Think We Know Things About Medical Professionals and Scientists
Ever hear about Ignác Semmelweis? He was the guy who figured out handwashing between surgeries and baby deliveries dramatically reduced patient mortality. But although Semmelweis had some data to prove the reduction in mortality, he didn't have any clear explanation as to why handwashing was helpful. So a rather large group of his peers decided they knew things, things Semmelweis, and those who agreed with him, didn't know. They mocked him. Details are sketchy but it may be that he suffered a nervous breakdown. He was

committed to an asylum where he was beaten and died two weeks after he was admitted. It was only years after his death that his ideas were recognized as truth.[8]

Similarly, Joseph Lister discovered sterilization of surgical instruments and cleaning wounds reduced infection and improved outcomes. Once again a large group of colleagues thought they knew things. They derided Lister for these ideas. Today we all know the difference sterilization makes.[9]

We Think We Know Things About the Accused

Yesterday, my grandson Andrew and I watched the movie *Stand and Deliver*. It's an excellent movie (based on a true story) about Jaime Escalante, a teacher who goes to work in a Los Angeles high school where the students are mainly poor Hispanic kids. He decides to teach them calculus as a means to help them escape the cycle of poverty. When the kids in his class all pass the AP Calculus exam they're accused of cheating.

So there's this one line in the movie where Escalante asks a school administrator if she thinks the kids cheated. She says, "You know, when I learn about someone who's accused of committing a crime, I think, most of the time: they did it. Don't you?" She wasn't alone in her assessment. There were others who were sure those kids cheated. They knew things.

But as you probably guessed, the poor Mexican kids didn't cheat. It was their investment of hard work and time that caused them to pass that test.[10]

There's another movie based on a true story about Richard Jewell. Jewell was the man who discovered a bomb during the 1996 Olympics in Atlanta, Georgia. He was accused by the FBI of planting that bomb. So many of us who read about Jewell in the media were sure he was guilty and we were angry about it. We knew things. But after Jewell's life was made a nightmare by the media and law enforcement, more information came to light and we found out we were wrong.[11]

Ananias Thought He Knew Things

In the passage quoted above, the Lord said to Ananias, "Rise and go to the street called Straight, and at the house of Judas look for a man of Tarsus named Saul . . ." But Ananias has heard things. And he hasn't just heard things from one person, but from many. And he tells God about what he's heard because he's afraid of Saul. Ananias is protesting against what God is telling Ananias to do. Because Ananias thinks he knows things.

The Only One Who Really Knows

So here's the thing. In all these instances, there's only one Person who really knows anything, and that Person is God. Everybody thought they knew Lindy killed her baby, but God knew she was innocent. Everybody thought they knew the Mexican kids cheated, but God knew they performed with integrity. Everybody thought they knew Richard Jewell planted that bomb, but God knew the truth was he saved lives by evacuating the crowd near the bomb.

The situation with Ananias is interesting because before he encountered Christ, Saul of Tarsus was sure the followers of the Way were ignorant misinformed heretics, and, Ananias thought he knew Saul was dangerous. But they were both wrong.

God knew His own Son was the Way, the Truth, and the Life. And God knew Saul was already far along in the process of being transformed from an enemy of Jesus into one of the greatest advocates of Jesus Christ in history. God knew Saul was anything but dangerous. God knew Saul was being transformed into Paul the Apostle.

The One Thing We Have in Common with Ananias

Imagine with me you're Ananias. And God tells you to go to a house where Saul is waiting for you. Saul, the one who was breathing murderous threats against Jesus' followers. Saul the one who voted for Stephen and other believers to be put to death. Saul who made it his life's mission to hunt down Christians. A self-declared enemy of Christians. If ever there was a time when righteous anger was justified, it was in that moment, when Ananias considered all the evil Saul had done.

But Ananias was wrong about Saul.

He didn't know what God was doing in Saul's heart and mind and soul.

And I'm the same—no—I'm certainly less than Ananias. In verse 10, Ananias is identified as a disciple of Jesus. I really feel like I'm someone who's *trying* to become a disciple of Jesus. When God called his name, Ananias said, "Here I am, Lord." When God calls my name I think I sometimes find ways to run and hide. So I'm definitely far less of a man than Ananias. But the way Ananias was enlightened by God about Saul makes me realize the one thing I have in common with Ananias is how little I know about others.

I might think I know what others are thinking. I might feel like I'm sure I know what they're going to do. I might feel positive I know what's in their heart. But the truth is, I don't. Like Ananias, I don't know what God is doing in the heart and mind and soul of others.

The family member who disagrees with me about COVID might be doing the very best they can, and — twenty years from now when we know more about this virus — that person might be right about some things that I was sure he or she was wrong about. The coworker

I've assigned a motive to might have something completely different in mind. The person I've identified as an enemy of Christ might be chosen by God to become one of the biggest advocates of Christianity in history for all I know.

Not Knowing and Jesus

So, where does that leave us?

We know we can't know what God knows. As I was studying this passage in Acts 9, I realized, if Ananias didn't know what was inside of a person like Saul of Tarsus, there's no way you and I can know what's inside of anyone. And because there's no way you and I can know what God is doing inside of anyone, and because only God *can* know, when you and I make assumptions about what someone is thinking or feeling, we're putting ourselves in the place of God.

I heard a nun talking about Mother Teresa the other day (in an online video). She said Mother Teresa and a friend were standing next to each other on the street when a mutual acquaintance approached them. This person who was walking toward them happened to be someone Mother Teresa found obnoxious. As the person drew nearer, Mother Teresa leaned toward her friend's ear and said in a quiet voice,

"Here comes Jesus in that annoying disguise."

So *this* is where God leaves us. This is where God leaves you and this is where God leaves me. Because we can't know what God is doing in the hearts and minds and souls of others, our only recourse is, to treat every person God puts in front of us (including people on the internet) just as though that person is Jesus.

119

I'm No One of Consequence

Finally, I want to point out I'm no one of consequence. I'm not a trained theologian. I have no authority in the church. And I've also come to appreciate what the church fathers have to say about anger. And their thoughts about anger trump mine. But even when I listen to well thought out arguments in favor of righteous anger from the best Bible teachers, the most favorable take on anger I can find is that 1) It's dangerous, because of our selfish sin nature. It can go wrong quickly. 2) It should be rare. 3) It should be on behalf of someone else. 4) And we should get rid of it quickly as we're instructed to in Ephesians 4:26.

In closing, I'll leave you with a couple of quotes from St. Francis de Sales, with whom I agree completely:

> *Most emphatically I say it, If possible, fall out with no one, and on no pretext whatever suffer your heart to admit anger and passion. Saint James says, plainly and unreservedly, that "the wrath of man worketh not the righteousness of God."*
> *St. Francis de Sales*

And:

> *Depend upon it, it is better to learn how to live without being angry than to imagine one can moderate and control anger lawfully; and if through weakness and frailty one is overtaken by it, it is far better to put it away forcibly than to parley with it; for give anger ever so little way, and it will become master, like the serpent, who easily works in its body wherever it can once introduce its head.*
> *St. Francis de Sales, Introduction to the Devout Life*

Notes:

1. Brant Hansen, *Unoffendable*, Thomas Nelson, 2015
2. J.I. Packer, *Knowing God*, IVP Books, 2011
3. Cleveland Clinic Heart and Vascular Team, *Angry Young Men and Heart Disease*, June 4, 2013, URL: https://health.clevelandclinic.org/2013/06/studies-show-angry-young-men-become-old-men-with-heart-disease/
4. Tony Dungy, *Do I Ever Get Angry? Yes and This is What I Do*, allprodad.com
5. Dr. Joe Martin, *4 Ways to Rise Above Anger*, https://www.realmenconnect.com/podcast
6. Chamberlain "Dingo" Trial 1982: https://famous-trials.com/dingo
7. The McDonald's Hot Coffee Case, https://www.caoc.org/?pg=facts
8. Ignác Semmelweis Wiki page: https://en.wikipedia.org/wiki/Ignaz_Semmelweis
9. Joseph Lister Wiki page: https://en.wikipedia.org/wiki/Joseph_Lister
10. *Stand and Deliver*, IMDb: https://www.imdb.com/title/tt0094027/
11. Richard Jewell, IMDb: https://www.imdb.com/title/tt3513548/

Joseph Scheumann, *Five Truths About the Wrath of God*, Desiring God, 11/4/2014

CHAPTER 19

Love Like Jesus

Jesus and the Charisma Myth

*If I speak in the tongues of men and of angels, but have
not love, I am a noisy gong or a clanging cymbal.*
1 CORINTHIANS 13:1

"Be Winsome"

"Be winsome," the pastor at the pulpit said to me, and to the rest of the congregation seated before him that Sunday morning. In context, he was instructing us to be winsome even as Jesus is winsome, so we can influence people for Christ more effectively. A year or so later I heard another pastor give the same exact instruction: "Be winsome."

I get it. Jesus was the most winsome person to ever walk the planet. He was charismatic beyond anyone in history. People were so attracted to him, at times the press of the crowd prevented him from eating. He was so charismatic they tried to make him king by force. He was so charismatic "Jesus could no longer openly enter a town . . . [because] people were coming to him from every quarter." Great multitudes followed him. As you read through the gospels, you see the word *multitude* used again and again. Jesus was winsome. Jesus had charisma more than any other. (Mark 3:20, John 6:15, Mark 1:45)

So, the pastor said:

"Be winsome," so we could be more like Jesus.

But for a socially clueless person like me—that advice wasn't particularly helpful.

Jesus and the Charisma Myth

That experience, hearing the advice to "be winsome" and not knowing how to follow that advice, was a large part of what inspired me to embark on this quest to learn how Jesus loved people. It was a large part of what inspired me to research what you're reading in this book. And that quest to learn how Jesus loved people (and how to be winsome so I could love more like Jesus) took me to an excellent book by Olivia Fox Cabane titled *The Charisma Myth*.[1]

The premise of *The Charisma Myth* is the common notion that "you're either born with charisma—or you're born without it" is a myth. In Cabane's book I learned how "in controlled laboratory experiments, researchers were able to raise and lower people's levels of charisma as if they were turning a dial."

Cabane describes how people perceive three qualities in charismatic people: power, warmth, and presence. As I read this, I couldn't help but think of Jesus and how he displays all three. Anyone who reads the gospels would say that Jesus' power, his warmth, and his presence are undeniable.

I also learned that through her research, Cabane has identified four different types of charisma.

~ Kindness charisma: Nelson Mandela was an example of a person with kindness charisma. Kindness charisma is warmth towards others. When you have this type of charisma, the people around you feel your goodwill toward them and your compassion for them.

~ Focus charisma: Mahatma Gandhi displayed this kind of charisma. His attention was very much in the moment. The person with focus charisma listens attentively and with an attitude of warmth.

~ Authority charisma: Authority charisma is why people listen to you and respond. When people recognize your authority, they *want* to listen. In a crisis, people respond to those who are bold, confident, and decisive. Colin Powell would be an example of someone with authority charisma.

~ Vision charisma: Martin Luther King Jr., Joan of Arc, and Elon Musk are people who had (or have) vision charisma. People with vision charisma have a powerful vision, and they communicate that vision with great conviction.

Oncured, Plauner, Lul Ahid

Again I thought of Jesus and how we see all four types of charisma in him. People who were used to being disparaged and dismissed by others were treated with kindness by Jesus. And Jesus displayed focus in his conversation with the woman at the well and in his interactions with his disciples. And he displayed authority when he gave commands and assignments to his followers. And when we read about the way he spoke, we see that he was the greatest communicator of vision there ever was.

How to Love Like Jesus

Right about now you might be thinking, "OK, so I get it. A lot of what you read in *The Charisma Myth* lined up with Jesus' charisma and winsomeness. So what?"

What I have found is that charisma helps me to communicate the love of Jesus. Because Jesus was obviously charismatic, the more charismatic I can be, the more I can effectively love like Jesus loved. *The Charisma Myth* helped me to be more charismatic, or to "be winsome" as my pastor instructed (at least more so than I used to be).

One discovery I found helpful was that it turns out you don't have to be an outgoing person to be charismatic. I'm an introvert, and I learned that introverts can actually have an advantage when it comes to certain kinds of charisma, like focus. When another person is speaking, the extrovert is often thinking about what he's going to say next, rather than being present in the moment and listening to what is being said. The introvert is better at listening and genuinely trying to understand what the other person is communicating.

I also found useful Cabane's insights concerning perceptions and what they can do to encourage or shut down the communication of the love of Jesus. To elaborate a bit more on focus charisma: If someone perceives disengagement on the part of another during an interpersonal interaction, they'll resent that person. So you might have the best intentions ever, but if the person you're interacting with perceives disengagement, it's unlikely that person will recognize your attempts to love like Jesus. It's the same with authenticity. If a person perceives you to be inauthentic, they'll be closed off from receiving love from you. "In fact, Stanford researchers conducted experiments showing that when people try to hide their feelings, they provoke a threat-response arousal in others." (Cabane)

I found this helpful because I used to think I could fake it. It turns out people recognize when you're pretending to pay attention or when you're pretending to be authentic. (This is just one of the of the reasons the chapter on the Holy Spirit is so important. Your love is never more authentic than when you're filled with the Holy Spirit.)

I learned that what we're instructed to do in 1 Thessalonians 5:18 increases charisma. That's right, gratitude increases charisma. So we can influence people for Jesus more effectively when we "Give thanks in all circumstances; for this is the will of God in Christ Jesus for you."

And I learned about charisma killers. Resentment, neediness, desperation, and offering unsolicited advice all kill charisma. You could say they're like noise that disrupts the music of winsomeness. As I read *The Charisma Myth* I realized it lines up with 1 Corinthians 13. If I "have not love, I am a noisy gong or a clanging cymbal." Meaningless

Not giving unsolicited advice was a hard one for me. I love to give advice! But one time I heard Bob Goff say something that really helped my with this problem. During an interview, Bob said he's never given anyone advice ever—he just shares observations. And I've noticed his observations are always about himself or someone other than the person he's talking to.[2]

In *The Charisma Myth*, Cabane also offers many practical and immediately applicable tools to increase your charisma. Here are three quick ones that will have an immediate effect.

~ Lower the intonation of your voice at the end of sentences.

~ Nod rarely, or not at all.

~ Pause a full two seconds before speaking. (Interrupting is a charisma killer—and letting others interrupt you is not.)

"Be Winsome" ~Appealing

I know some might complain that I'm inserting science into a book about the Jesus of the Bible. But if we're to love like Jesus as he commanded us to in John 15:12, and if Jesus loved with great charisma, then it only makes sense for you and me to become as charismatic as we can. Not for the purpose of attracting people to ourselves, but for the purpose of attracting people to Jesus.

And if we're offered tools that can raise our level of charisma as if we were turning a dial, then we should use those tools, for God's glory.

So to love like Jesus, "be winsome" like Jesus.

Be more charismatic like Jesus.

Turn up the dial.

Notes

1. Olivia Fox Cabane, *The Charisma Myth: How Anyone Can Master the Art and Science of Personal Magnetism*, Portfolio, 2012
2. Interview with Bob and Maria Goff, Carey Nieuwhof Leadership Podcast CNLP 138, URL: https://careynieuwhof.com/episode138/

Break - back
- Alun w/ girls - meeting him
Nvls, d woul
- mid - w/gul Sulgs - distraught
exhausted

128

Part Three

Foundational Practices of Jesus

CHAPTER 20

Love Like Jesus

Love God First

How Jesus Loved God

Jesus loved God so much, he didn't assign value to what other people thought of him. We see it when he healed on the Sabbath even though he knew the religious leaders would be offended. We see it when he spoke about eating his body and drinking his blood when he knew it would mean losing most of his followers. We see it when he overturned the tables of the money changers in the temple even though he knew the Pharisees would disapprove. Jesus expressed his love for God in these ways, without regard for the opinions of the people around him. (John 12:9–14, John 6:56–66, John 2:14–15)

Jesus loved God so much that he desired to obey him even when it meant torture, and death on the cross.

The Supreme Weapon

Josef Tson was a pastor in Romania during a time of Christian persecution. He lived in hiding until one day the Romanian government captured and tortured him. The following is an exchange he had with one of his interrogators.

Josef Tson to his Romanian interrogator:

"Sir, let me explain how I see this issue. Your supreme weapon is killing. My supreme weapon is dying. Here is how it works. You know that my sermons on tape have spread all over the country. If you kill me, those sermons will be sprinkled with my blood. Everyone will know I died for my preaching. And everyone who has a tape will pick it up and say, 'I'd better listen again to what this man preached, because he really meant it: he sealed it with his life.' So, sir, my sermons will speak ten times louder than before. I will actually rejoice in this supreme victory if you kill me."

After this encounter, Tson found out another officer said, "We know that Mr. Tson would love to be a martyr, but we are not that foolish to fulfill his wish."

Tson said, "I stopped to consider the meaning of that statement. I remembered how for many years, I had been afraid of dying. I had kept a low profile. Because I wanted badly to live, I had wasted my life in inactivity. But now that I had placed my life on the altar and decided I was ready to die for the gospel, they were telling me they would not kill me! I could go wherever I wanted in the country and preach whatever I wanted, knowing I was safe."

"As long as I tried to save my life, I was losing it. Now that I was willing to lose it, I found it."[1]

How to Love Like Jesus

Jesus knew what others would think of his words and his actions. He knew what they would do to him. But He expressed his love for his God anyway.

In John 2:23–25 we learn how "many believed in his name when they saw the signs that he was doing. But Jesus on his part did not entrust himself to them, because he knew all people . . . for he himself knew what was in man."

Jesus loved God first, and he loved Him with abandon. He gave no value to what others thought of him with regard to his love for his God. Even when it meant the Pharisees would become so offended they would torture him, and kill him.

One of the most important keys to loving like Jesus is to love God first in this way. To love Him far above anyone else. This is the idea behind Jesus' teaching: "If anyone comes to me and does not hate his own father and mother and wife and children and brothers and sisters, yes, and even his own life, he cannot be my disciple." (Luke 14:26) Obviously Jesus taught over and over again that we are to love God and love people, and of course that includes the people in your family. What he's saying in Luke 14, and what we see Jesus demonstrating when he heals on the Sabbath, and speaks inspired words that offend, and when he cleanses the temple, is to love God first, far above anyone else. Jesus cares deeply about what God thinks, and what pleases Him. And He puts that above, far above, what other people think.

When I put God first, I'm blessed because I become focused on what's truly important in life. When God slips out of first place, I quickly become mired down in the temporal. My heart and my soul and my mind are taken up with what friends and family think. Or what my co-workers think. Or what I feel is expected of me by the culture I live in. And a kind of inertia sets in. The more I move in the direction of the temporal expectations of the people around me, the farther away I drift from God and the eternal. In my experience, when I find myself in this state of being, I'm usually brought back to intimacy with God through some sort of crisis. You can learn from experience, but it doesn't have to be your own experience. Let me encourage you to learn from mine. Put God first and draw close to God before the crisis comes.

Shame and Embarrassment

There have been times in my life when I was skulking around, embarrassed about my love for Christ. I lived in fear of what others might think of me. I'm on dangerous ground when I live like that. Jesus said plainly, "I tell you, everyone who acknowledges me before men, the Son of Man also will acknowledge before the angels of God, but the one who denies me before men will be denied before the angels of God." (Luke 12:8–9)

I don't know about you, but I don't want to be disowned by Christ before the angels of God.

What it comes down to concerning this issue of shame is that each one of us is presented with the same choice as Josef Tson. We're facing death—and we're afraid of dying. Not a physical death, but a social one. We're afraid if we sell out for Jesus Christ we'll lose friends, or at the very least, suffer embarrassment. But in the end, we have the same choice as Tson. We can keep a low profile, and waste our lives with inactivity for Christ, or we can place our lives on the altar, and decide we're ready to die for Him.

Like Josef Tson, once you decide you're ready to die for Christ, socially speaking in your case and mine, you're free. I've experienced this myself and observed it in others. There will be awkwardness during the transition, but tell me what transition is without awkwardness. And tell me of anything in life worthwhile that doesn't require transition.

Like Josef Tson, you'll be amazed at the freedom you enjoy, once you decide to place your life on the altar. Once you give yourself over to Christ.

So don't be afraid of dying. Josef Tson said, "As long as I tried to save my life, I was losing it. Now that I was willing to lose it, I found it."

That's how it will be for you, when you decide to love God with abandon. That's how it will be for you when you give your life over to Jesus completely.

When you love God the same way Jesus did: far more than anyone else, with abandon, giving no value to what others think of you with regard to your love for God,

That's when you'll find you're truly free.

> *For whoever would save his life will lose it, but whoever loses his life for my sake will find it.*
> *Jesus Christ, Matthew 16:25*

Notes:
1. Original source for Josef Tson story: ToEveryTribe.com, Fall 2009 Newsletter (This story is no longer available on the To Every Tribe website. You can read another version on Baptist Press: Romanian Josef Tson recounts God's grace amid suffering, 7/19/2004)

CHAPTER 21

Love Like Jesus

Find Friends Like Jesus

The Angry Crowd

I was sitting in class with about thirty-five other people on a Friday afternoon at the National Fire Academy in Maryland near Washington, D.C. Before our instructor dismissed us, he warned us to avoid downtown D.C. that weekend because there was going to be a large pro-life demonstration happening there.

What happened next nearly knocked me off my chair. Just as soon as the words "pro-life" passed his lips, the class erupted with loud jeers and boos from almost everyone in the room. The contempt for anyone with a pro-life viewpoint was palpable.

Like you, I think of myself as independent of and unconstrained by the thinking of the people around me. But during the jeers and boos, I looked over at my friend sitting next to me and hoped to God he didn't say anything that would tip the crowd concerning my pro-life sentiments. I feared the intense disapproval of my classmates. I was afraid I would be shunned. My normally solid convictions wavered.

"Was there some way I could compromise my beliefs so I could avoid being ostracized by my classmates?" I thought to myself.

Criticism, Pushback, and Misunderstanding

One time when Jesus was teaching and healing in Galilee, he was intentionally staying away from Judea. He stayed away because of the threat from the Pharisees. Because he had been healing people on the Sabbath, and because he declared himself to be God's own Son, the Pharisees were offended. They used these reasons to justify their plot to murder Jesus (although envy and a desire to preserve their own power base were the true roots of their motivation). During Jesus' time on earth, Galilee and Judea were under separate jurisdictions, so remaining in Galilee was a means for Jesus to stay out of harm's way.[1]

But then the time came for the Feast of Booths, a feast that was celebrated for eight days in Jerusalem, which was in the jurisdiction of Judea where Jesus' enemies resided. Jewish families and even entire Jewish neighborhoods from all over would travel together to Jerusalem for this feast. So Jesus' (half) brothers are going and, as brothers sometimes do, they goad him. In a provocative way, they tell Jesus what he should do. They criticize him for remaining in the relatively obscure community of Galilee. And they give him the marketing wisdom of the day: Go to a major population center so you can promote yourself. Verse 5 confirms their provocative tone. "For not even his brothers believed in him." (John 7:5)

Jesus' biological half-brothers didn't get him. Jesus was operating in the Spirit while his brothers were just doing whatever the rest of the Jewish community was doing.

Another time we read that Jesus' family tried to physically remove him from the press of a great crowd he was ministering to. At that time his family actually said, "He is out of his mind." (Mark 3:20–21)

Later in that same chapter, they tell Jesus that his mother and brothers want to see him. And Jesus responded, "Who are my mother and my brothers?" And looking around at those who were with him, he said, "Here are my mother and my brothers." (See Mark 3:31–35.)

Something I discovered is when you start to live a life of loving like Jesus there will be criticism, pushback, and misunderstanding, sometimes from people you would never expect, including family and religious people. For that reason alone you'll need strength from God, and you'll need strength from the people around you.

What Science Has Identified as One of the Most Powerful Forces on Earth

One of the most powerful forces on earth is something called social norming. It works like this: Each one of us believes with all our heart, and with all our soul, and with all our mind that "I am my own man," or, "I am my own woman." Each of us likes to think: "While others may be susceptible to the influence of those they surround themselves with, I think for myself."

But over and over again science says otherwise. You can hear it in a podcast from the experts at Freakonomics.[2] You can read about it from Arizona State University professor Dr. Robert Cialdini.[3] You can learn about it in research cited by Malcolm Gladwell.[4] The influence of those we surround ourselves with is consistently underestimated. But it turns out it's one of the most powerful forces there is when it comes to what determines our thinking and behavior.

How Jesus Loved People: Jesus' Two Families

So when Jesus looks around at those who were with him and says, "Here are my mother and my brothers," what does he mean?

When we read the gospels, we see that although Jesus befriended many sinners, he surrounded himself with a core group of people, each of whom loved God with all his heart and with all his soul and with all his mind. Each of them loved people as themselves. And each of them was wholly committed to Jesus himself. These lovers of God and people became Jesus' family. They were the ones he lived with, day in and day out, for three years.

How to Love Like Jesus: Your Two Families

Ponder this for a moment: Jesus Christ, *the Son of God*, *the Light of the World*, he surrounded himself with people who loved God with all their heart, soul, and mind. Recognizing the obvious, that you and I are far less than he is:

For you and for me to love like Jesus, we need to choose our inner circle like Jesus.

To determine who he would choose, Jesus "went out to the mountain to pray, and all night he continued in prayer to God. And when day came, he called his disciples and chose from them twelve, whom he named apostles." (Luke 6:12–13)

The best way for you and me to choose our inner circle is to prayerfully and purposefully determine who our core group will be, the same way Jesus determined his. Choose an inner circle who will influence you to love God and people. Choose a core group who are wholly committed to Jesus Christ.

Tim Ferriss, the author of the book *Tools of Titans*, was asked, "If you could have a billboard in a location with the greatest possible visibility, what would you put on that billboard?" And his answer was:

Find Friends Like Jesus

You are the average of the five people you most associate with.[5]

For good or for bad, one of the most powerful forces on earth is the force of social norming. You can use it for good.

If *you* want to love like Jesus, find *people* who love like Jesus and surround yourself with them. Find people who love God and Jesus with everything they have. You'll usually find them doing something for God's kingdom. Often you'll find them in a church. Unfortunately, there are plenty of churches filled with people just going through the motions—lukewarm churches. And there are even churches filled with people worshipping something other than God. (I recently saw a video of a sermon encouraging people to come to church so they could make more money.) But there are also churches with Christ followers who love God with all their heart, and with all their soul, and with all their mind. Find those people. Look first in places where people are doing something for God's kingdom. Find out what they're doing and go do it with them. Get to know them. Ask around. Research reviews of ministries and churches on the internet. Volunteer with different ministries for a few hours per month. Try different churches. Don't be afraid to fail. Don't fear trial and error. Who you surround yourself with will be one of the most important decisions of your entire life. Jesus himself prayed all night about this decision.

Don't stop until you find the people who love God and who love people, like Jesus.

Do whatever you have to do to find these people and make them your core group.

That's what Jesus did.

You do it too.

Notes:

Further study on the amazing power of social norming will be rewarded. I recommend the Freakonomics podcast, "Riding the Herd Mentality," from 6/21/2012, Robert Cialdini's excellent book *Influence: The Psychology of Persuasion*, and Malcolm Gladwell's article, "Do Parents Matter?," 8/17/1998.

1. Craig S. Keener, *The IVP Bible Background Commentary: New Testament*, InterVarsity Press, 1993
2. Stephen Dubner, "Riding the Herd Mentality," Freakonomics Podcast, 6/21/2012
3. Robert B. Cialdini Ph.D., *Influence: The Psychology of Persuasion*, Harper Business, 12/26/2006
4. Malcolm Gladwell, "Do Parents Matter?," 8/17/1998
5. Melia Robinson, Tim Ferriss: "You are the average of the five people you most associate with," Business Insider, 1/11/2017

Albert Mohler, "Rethinking Secularization: A Conversation with Peter Berger," albertmohler.com, 10/11/2010
Anthony Lising, School of Education, Stanford University, "The Influence of Friendship Groups on Intellectual Self-Confidence and Educational Aspirations in College"

CHAPTER 22

Love Like Jesus

Jesus and the Holy Spirit

And John bore witness: "I saw the Spirit descend from heaven like a dove, and it remained on him. I myself did not know him, but he who sent me to baptize with water said to me, 'He on whom you see the Spirit descend and remain, this is he who baptizes with the Holy Spirit.' And I have seen and have borne witness that this is the Son of God."

JOHN 1:32–34

We know very little about Jesus' life before the event recorded in the passage above. We know something of his birth. And we know about the time his parents lost track of him when he was twelve years old, when he was dialoguing with the rabbis in the temple. But that's it. There's no record of Jesus performing miracles before the Holy Spirit descended upon him like a dove. Maybe you're like me and you've wondered if there was some reason behind the change in Jesus' life at the beginning of his public work for God's kingdom. If you've wondered, read on.

Did Jesus Need the Holy Spirit?

Perhaps you have heard it before, that when Jesus came to this planet, he left all of his personal divine power behind in heaven. I can't say for certain whether that's true or not. There are theologians on both sides of the issue. But we do have Philippians 2:7 that says Jesus "emptied himself, by taking the form of a servant, being born in the likeness of men." (See also Hebrews 2:9.) And as we saw in the paragraphs above, what we *can* say, is that it wasn't until this moment, the moment in our passage where John the Baptist describes how he saw the Spirit descend onto Jesus from heaven like a dove, that the record of Jesus' teaching and miracles begins.

So it would appear that it was necessary for God's Holy Spirit to be poured out upon Jesus, in order for him to do all the amazing works we see him do in the gospels. Which begs the question: If Jesus needed to be baptized with God's Holy Spirit, how much more do you, and how much more do I?

Should You Ask for God's Holy Spirit?

It's clear the apostles thought every believer should be baptized with the Holy Spirit. We see that when they encountered people who believed in Jesus but didn't yet know about the baptism with the Holy Spirit in Acts 8:14–17.

> *. . . Peter and John, who came down and prayed for them that they might receive the Holy Spirit, for he had not yet fallen on any of them, but they had only been baptized in the name of the Lord Jesus. Then they laid their hands on them and they received the Holy Spirit.*
> *Acts 8:14–24*

So scripture indicates that it's God's will for His Holy Spirit to be poured out upon every Christ follower. And we see that John the Baptist says in our text at the beginning of this chapter, Jesus the Son of God will baptize with the Holy Spirit. (John 1:33–34)

"But how?" you might be asking right now. "How do I receive the baptism of God's Holy Spirit?"

How to Receive the Holy Spirit

Jesus tells us how. He says, "What father among you, if his son asks for a fish, will instead of a fish give him a serpent; or if he asks for an egg, will give him a scorpion? If you then, who are evil, know how to give good gifts to your children, how much more will the heavenly Father give the Holy Spirit to those who ask him!" (Luke 11:11–13)

So we're to ask. That's it: just ask. And then in Luke chapter 18 Jesus even tells us how to ask.

And he told them a parable to the effect that they ought always to pray and not lose heart. He said, "In a certain city there was a judge who neither feared God nor respected man. And there was a widow in that city who kept coming to him and saying, 'Give me justice against my adversary.' For a while he refused, but afterward he said to himself, 'Though I neither fear God nor respect man, yet because this widow keeps bothering me, I will give her justice, so that she will not beat me down by her continual coming.'" And the Lord said, "Hear what the unrighteous judge says. And will not God give justice to his elect, who cry to him day and night? Will he delay long over them? I tell you, he will give justice to them speedily. Nevertheless, when the Son of Man comes, will he find faith on earth?"

Luke 18:1–8

This is how the disciples prayed after Jesus ordered them to wait in Jerusalem for the promise of God's Holy Spirit. Jesus said, "you heard from me; for John baptized with water, but you will be baptized with the Holy Spirit not many days from now." (Acts 1:4–5) After Jesus said these words the disciples "with one accord were devoting themselves to prayer, together with the women and Mary the mother of Jesus, and his brothers." (Acts 1:14) The disciples petitioned God as the widow petitioned the unrighteous judge in the parable. And to see how God responded, just have a look at Acts chapter 2. There we see as a result of the disciples receiving the Holy Spirit, three thousand people responded to their message and gave themselves to Jesus.

Why Not Ask Right Now?

So do as Jesus instructed you and me to do. Ask God for His Holy Spirit to be poured out upon you. Ask as Jesus' disciples asked. Ask like the widow asked the unrighteous judge. Ask right now. Ask again tomorrow. Ask at the start of every day. Ask three times a day.

The Holy Spirit manifests differently in different people, and in my experience, it can be difficult to see the Holy Spirit working in your life overtly. However, I believe you can still know whether or not you have the Holy Spirit in the way the disciples did in Acts chapter 2. Just ask in the way Jesus instructed us to ask. Ask in this way and you can be sure you'll receive God's Holy Spirit in the same way you can be sure you're saved. You know you're saved because you believe God's words in John 3:16. In the same way, you can know you'll receive God's Holy Spirit because you believe Jesus' words when he said, your heavenly Father will give His Holy Spirit to those who ask Him. (See Luke 11:11–13.)

For Jesus to love the way he did, he needed God's Holy Spirit to be poured out upon him.

You and I do too.

So ask.

CHAPTER 23

Love Like Jesus

Jesus and the Fluid Life

*So when the Samaritans came to him, they asked him
to stay with them, and he stayed there two days.*

JOHN 4:40

How Jesus Loved People

Jesus was on his way to Galilee when he encountered the woman
at the well. It should have been just a short break for water and
maybe a little food before continuing on to his scheduled destination,
but that's not how it worked out.

His Holy Spirit led conversation there at the well, led to the people
of that Samaritan town to ask him to stay. So, he did. For two days
Jesus shared the words of eternal life with the Samaritan townspeople.

How to Love Like Jesus

I love the way Jesus describes the Holy Spirit as living water because when we're led by the Holy Spirit, our lives often become fluid. (John 7:37–39)

I used to live a life that was just the opposite. I was scheduled to "maximize my productivity." I scheduled activity after activity, meeting after meeting, appointment after appointment, both professionally and personally. My motivation was sincere. I wanted to be as productive as possible. But without realizing it, I left no room for the Holy Spirit to direct my life. How could He? I didn't have a minute to spare.

Overscheduling yourself is a great way to kill the Holy Spirit's influence in your life, and His corresponding fruit, which is loving like Jesus.

Jesus didn't live that way. Here he is, the most important person on the planet, on a trip to Galilee, and, following the direction of the Holy Spirit, he takes two whole days out of His schedule to talk with the Samaritans.

Can you imagine someone important today, say a CEO or the POTUS, spontaneously taking two days out of his schedule to talk to one small group of ordinary people? It would never happen. Most people I observe in our culture don't leave room to live a fluid, Spirit-filled life. They like to keep busy. They have things to do. And when the Holy Spirit presents opportunity, they usually don't respond, because there's nearly always a previous commitment. Stop and talk with the lonely awkward guy at church? Can't, gotta lunch date right after. Share the Lord with the newly divorced guy at work? Can't, gotta make softball practice. Invite the unsaved friend to Bible study? Can't, too much already going on that day. This doesn't describe a life led by the Holy Spirit.

A life led by the Holy Spirit is a life that's flexible, free, and fluid. When you choose to live such a life, you're in for both good news, and bad.

The Good News

If you live this flexible life, you can love people like Jesus did, that's the good news. Availability, flexibility, fluidity translates into opportunity for the Holy Spirit to direct you to love people. To love people like Jesus loved people.

The Bad News

The bad news is, some people don't deal well with spontaneity. When you live this way, you'll be misunderstood. Some will say you lack discipline. Some might think you're flaky. Some will become upset with you. That can be tough to take. Especially when some of those people are people you care about. Some might come from your church. Some might even come from your own family. It's absolutely essential you respond to those people with God's love and grace. And I think the more diligently you guard your heart, the better you'll handle those who misunderstand your Spirit-led life. (We'll address guarding your heart in the next chapter, Guard Your Heart Like Jesus.

In the end though, it's worth it. Yes, you'll come under criticism for what some will perceive to be a disregard for structure, but the fruit that's born makes it all worth it. Look what happened when Jesus loved this way, many of the Samaritans from that town believed.

So to love like Jesus, live a life that's flexible, free, and fluid.

Jesus did.

You can too.

The natural person does not accept the things of the Spirit of God, for they are folly to him, and he is not able to understand them because they are spiritually discerned.

1 Corinthians 2:14

CHAPTER 24

Love Like Jesus

Guard Your Heart Like Jesus

So he came to a town of Samaria called Sychar . . . Jacob's well was there; so Jesus, wearied as he was from his journey, was sitting beside the well. It was about the sixth hour. A woman from Samaria came to draw water. Jesus said to her, "Give me a drink." (For his disciples had gone away into the city to buy food.)
JOHN 4:5–8

How Jesus Loved People: Diet, Rest, and Exercise

Jesus took care of Himself.

"What's that?" you're asking, "Jesus took care of himself? So what? What does that have to do with loving people?"

That's a great question.

Here, in this passage of scripture, we see Jesus, *the Son of God, the image of the invisible God, the firstborn over all creation*, taking care of himself. He's just finished exercising, if you will, as he walked to the town of Sychar. He's about to take in fluids, as he asked for a drink of water. He's mindful of his diet, as he sent his disciples to buy food. And we see that when he became weary, he rested as he sat by the well. (John 4:5–8, Colossians 1:15)

It is a rather curious thing to see he *who is and who was and who is to come, the Almighty*, taking care of himself.

How to Love Like Jesus:
Maybe you're like me and you feel like taking care of yourself is selfish. If you are, you might be interested in this story.

When I was in my early forties, I wasn't living like Jesus. I wasn't taking time to go for a walk through Samaria because I didn't have time to walk or exercise. I wasn't taking time to ask anyone to refresh me with water. I didn't send anyone to buy food, I was living so fast, I only had time to hit the drive-through—for fast food. I wasn't taking time to sit down by the well, I wasn't resting.

I was full of energy and bent on squeezing every minute out of my schedule every day. I took on extra responsibility at the fire department, I signed up as an elder at my church, I hosted a home church group, I taught a men's Bible study on leadership once a week, I built a house and contracted it myself, my wife and I started a vacation rental business, I went to school for my Bachelors in Fire Administration, I started writing a book.

I was working hard to get things done. Diet, exercise, rest? "I'll worry about those things after I'm dead," I always thought.

Well—death was very nearly the result of that lifestyle. One night after a Fire Administration class in Portland, Oregon, I was crossing the street to go to the Lloyd Center Mall. Suddenly I found it hard to breathe. I honestly thought I walked into an invisible hazardous materials cloud of some kind. The only problem with that theory was, nobody else around me was having a problem.

Next thing I knew, I was in the hospital for a double bypass operation.

God decided to downgrade my level of capability.

It turns out it was a big downgrade. Gone was all that energy. Some days I felt completely exhausted by ten in the morning. But do you think I changed my approach to life? I took a promotion at work. I continued to pursue my Bachelor's degree. I bought another vacation rental. I continued my involvement at church. I finished my book.

Needless to say, things didn't work out very well. Drained of my physical and mental resources, I had trouble just functioning, let alone performing at a high level. I fell into a depression which, of course, made things even worse. I struggled in every area of my life: spiritual, work, family, all of it. I suffered, and so did my relationships. I wasn't loving people like Jesus. I simply didn't have the energy to.

I wonder how things might have been different had I taken care of myself.

Jesus didn't live like I did. Jesus, *the Power of God* and *the radiance of God's glory*, walked. (1 Corinthians 1:24, Hebrews 1:3) He took fluids. He ate. He rested. He observed the Sabbath. He even took naps. (See Luke 8:23.) The emphasis of this chapter is on the physical, but Jesus guarded his heart in other important ways also. He surrounded himself with people who loved God with everything they had. He spent time in lonely places going deep in his relationship with our Father in heaven. He spent time in the scriptures. He prayed for, and followed the leading of, the Holy Spirit. These aspects of guarding your heart are covered in other chapters. The point is Jesus made sure he was in good condition to love people. Jesus followed the wisdom found in Proverbs 4:23 (NIV):

Above all else, guard your heart, for everything you do flows from it.

Maybe the Most Undervalued Verse in the Bible

The writer of Proverbs chapter 4 is sharing wisdom with his sons. He spends much of the chapter admonishing them to listen to his words and to value wisdom highly. Then toward the end, he writes, "Above all else, guard your heart . . ."

"Above all else," he wrote.

This instruction, which at the very least is the most important part of Proverbs 4, is something I've overlooked until recently. It's something you can learn right now. You don't have to wait until you've damaged relationships and have a health crisis like I did.

I used to spend a lot of time focused on being productive, at work, at home, in every area of my life. And while there's nothing wrong with being productive, too often, at the end of the day, I had an impressive number of items completed from my to-do list, but my heart was depleted. It was so depleted, I was unable to even begin to reflect Jesus in my relationships. In some cases, I caused serious damage to relationships, usually without realizing it until much later. The reason I failed God, family, and friends in this way was that I didn't guard my heart as the writer in Proverbs instructs us to. "Above all else," he said.

Here's what I failed to do:

I didn't spend enough time in community with people who loved Jesus with all their hearts, and all their minds, and all their souls.

I didn't spend enough time alone with Jesus in prayer.

I didn't give thanks enough. (See Philippians 4:6–7.)

I didn't spend enough time in God's word.

I didn't spend enough time sleeping. (Remember, even Jesus took naps.) (Mark 4:38)

I didn't eat a healthy diet.

I didn't spend enough time exercising.

I didn't build margin into my schedule.

I undervalued the Sabbath rhythm God wants us to enjoy.

And I'm sorry to say I'm not alone. The Christian community is full of people who live the same way, and what flows from our hearts is profoundly affected.

Everything Flows from Your Heart

"Everything you do flows from it." Everything you do flows from your heart, the writer of Proverbs says. When you don't guard your heart, the people around you drink in whatever flows out of it. If your heart is bitter, the flow is bitter. If your heart is angry or toxic, the flow is toxic.

The sad part is, I used to think I could fake it. "If I say the right things," I thought, "If I smile," I thought, "If I pretend to be attentive," I thought, "If I drink enough caffeine!" then I can get by, then I'll be okay. But I was wrong. I'm embarrassed to say that it wasn't that long ago I realized most people can tell when you're not authentic. I learned from my own mistakes in this area, if you're perceived by someone to be inauthentic, it becomes impossible for that person to feel loved by you.

In other words, nearly everybody can tell when it's not from your heart.

When you don't guard your heart, Jesus, who lives in the heart of the Christian, becomes unrecognizable to others.

It's Not Easy Being Me

My heart is particularly difficult to guard. I know people with hearts that seem to pour out Christ's love even when they're exhausted, or hungry, or too sedentary, or even in a very difficult circumstance that would cause most people to fall into depression.

I'm not one of those people. (And I'm guessing you're not either. That type of person is rare.)

If I don't spend time with people who love Jesus with everything they have, if I don't spend at least one half hour a day alone with our Father in prayer, if I don't give thanks often, if I don't study God's word, if I don't sleep enough, if I don't exercise every day, I'm not fit to be around people, let alone love like Jesus.

How to Love Like Jesus

We live in a culture where busy-ness is worshipped. So if you feel like taking care of yourself is selfish, you're not alone. And it *is* true, it *is* selfish to maintain yourself—when maintaining is your end goal. We see many people today who are obsessed with their diet or their sleep rhythms or their exercise.

But the point of taking care of yourself is so you can love God more deeply. The point of taking care of yourself is so you can love people more fully. So you can do more for Jesus. So you can become a sharper instrument to be used, by Him, for His purposes. So you can love like Jesus loved:

That's not selfish.

You and I might think we'll bear more fruit for God by using every minute we can to be "productive," but that's a trap. When I'm too busy, or too tired, or too burned out, I don't love well.

It's better to do less and reflect the nature of Christ, than it is to accomplish more in an un-Christlike manner.

All Jesus had to do was save the world within about a three-year time period, yet there's not one verse describing him as in a hurry.

Jesus guarded his heart.

"Above all else," the writer of Proverbs said. Prioritize it, he said.

Prioritize the guarding of your heart.

Guard your heart.

Guard it diligently.

To love like Jesus, do whatever you have to, to guard your heart—so what flows from your heart is the love of Jesus.

It's one of God's most important instructions.

CHAPTER 25

Love Like Jesus

Go Deep Like Jesus

*And rising very early in the morning, while it was
still dark, he departed and went out to a desolate place,
and there he prayed. And Simon and those who were
with him searched for him, and they found him and
said to him, "Everyone is looking for you." And he
said to them, "Let us go on to the next towns, that I
may preach there also, for that is why I came out."*

MARK 1:35–38

How Jesus Loved People

"Let us go on to the next towns," Jesus said. Jesus loved people by going somewhere. He went to nearby villages throughout Galilee, teaching and helping and healing.

But what about before that?

What did he do to prepare himself—to teach, and to heal, and to love people?

How to Love Like Jesus

I confess, I've had many gods over my lifetime. For most of the time my kids were growing up, my kids were my god. Then when they left the nest, my wife was my god. Then basketball, then tennis, then my real estate portfolio, then my job. Of course, none of these things are evil in any way, but each was my very top priority at one time or another. Each had a place as the ultimate in my life, ahead of Jesus.

In our text at the beginning of this chapter, we see that Jesus left the house and found a quiet place, where he prayed. His friends went to look for him, and when they found him, they said, "Everyone is looking for you."

If everyone were looking for you, where would they find you?

Would they find you away from the house, in a solitary place, praying, or reading God's scriptures?

Or would they find you with family, or on the golf course, or playing your favorite online game, or on Instagram, or surfing Reddit, or watching football?

If people don't find you going deep in your relationship with God, in the way Jesus did, people won't find you loving people like Jesus did either.

Consider this: If the Son of God, the Savior of the world, the Messiah Himself carved out deep times with His God before serving Him, how much more do you and I need to?

A person will carve out time to spend with his god. The only question is: Who or what is your god? What is it for you? Is it shopping, or golf, or a video game, or Twitter, or Snapchat, or ESPN, or money? Whatever your god is, I'm guessing you carve out time for it, right?

Or is your God the same God as Jesus' God? The way to tell is to take an honest look at where your time is spent, where your energy goes, where your money winds up.

Your God is where you invest yourself.

To love people, Jesus first loved his God, by investing himself in his God, in the morning, in a solitary place, one-on-one with Him.

For you it might be a walk alone in the morning (my personal favorite), or lying on your face on the floor in a quiet room, or before even getting up lying in bed to pray looking at the ceiling, or locking yourself in the bathroom (sometimes necessary—as a last resort). However you withdraw to your desolate place, the point is that before you can love like Jesus, you must love God in the way Jesus did.

To love people like Jesus, do what he did. Go to a solitary place, be alone with God, just you and Him. Pray to Him, pray with Him, read His words written to you.

Then go and love people.

> *Jesus often withdrew to lonely places and prayed.*
> *Luke 5:16 (NIV)*

CHAPTER 26

Love Like Jesus

Stay Faithful Like Jesus

When I married my wife, I had hardly a smidgen of
sense for what I was getting into with her. How could
I know how much she would change over 25 years?
How could I know how much I would change? My
wife has lived with at least five different men since
we were wed—and each of the five has been me.
The connecting link with my old self has always been the
memory of the name I took on back there: "I am he who
will be there with you." When we slough off that name,
lose that identity, we can hardly find ourselves again.

LEWIS SMEDES

How Jesus Loves People

Jesus loves people by staying faithful. Jesus remains faithful to you, and to me. Jesus loves *us*, by staying faithful, to the bride of Christ. When Jesus died on the cross, he entered into a covenant relationship with you and with me. He said to us, "You are My bride, and I am your Groom, and I will never leave you or forsake you—ever." (See Revelation 21:9, 19:7–9, 21:2, Isaiah 54:5, Ephesians 5:25, Matthew 28:20, Deuteronomy 31:8.)

Jesus did that even though I'm not a very attractive bride. I'm on the better end of the relationship, without question. Jesus sacrificed his position in heaven with his Father to dwell here on earth, for you and for me. He endured the ridicule of society, for you and for me. He endured unjust accusation and conviction in the courts, for you and for me. He endured the scourging with the cat-o'-nine-tails, he endured the thorny crown, he endured the nails penetrating his limbs, he endured the cross and the shame, for us. He endured all that for his bride's benefit—for your benefit, and for mine. He gave himself for our relationship. And what do I contribute, to our relationship? What little good I do doesn't begin to compare with His contributions. And the bad I do: So often, I do things that are unattractive to my Groom.

But still: He said He will never leave me nor forsake me. And He's One who does what He says He'll do. He will stay faithful to His Bride. So you should stay faithful to your spouse, and I should stay faithful to my spouse too. Except—there's this problem.

Help, I'm Married to a Stranger

> *The primary problem is . . . learning how to love and care for the stranger to whom you find yourself married.*
> -Stanley Hauerwas, Professor of Ethics, Duke University

Timothy and Kathy Keller, in their excellent book *The Meaning of Marriage*, write about the stranger we eventually find ourselves married to. Most of the material in this chapter comes from their book.[1] It's impossible to know what your spouse will be like tomorrow, or next year, or next decade. Because life will change him, or her. University changes him. Age changes her. Where she lives changes her. A loved one dying changes her. Having kids changes him. The hirings, and firings, and battles at work change him. You can't really know who you will be married to, in the future, because they'll change.

It's inevitable: At some point in your marriage, you'll find yourself married to a stranger. It happens to every one of us.

It happened to Jacob right away. You know the story. Jacob worked for Laban for seven years so he could have the hand of his daughter Rachel in marriage. She was physically beautiful and the one woman who held Jacob's heart. Rachel was worth every drop of sweat, every hour in the hot sun, every long day of toil. Year in and year out he worked, until, finally, after seven years, the time came and Laban had to pay up. Jacob was beside himself with anticipation. He entered the tent of his bride on their wedding night, but the next morning he woke up beside Leah. He was livid. What happened was, Laban wanted to marry off his oldest daughter Leah, but Laban had a problem: Leah was lacking in physical beauty. So Laban slipped her into the ceremony, in place of Rachel—bait-and-switch.

Jacob found himself married to a stranger. He would have to work another seven years before he was permitted to marry Rachel. (Genesis chapter 29)

Why Did You Choose Who You Chose to Marry?

Why did you choose her, or him? Did you think you found your soulmate? Were you looking for fulfillment? Were you hoping for a person who would help you live out your dreams? If you were, when that day comes, the day you wake up next to the stranger, and you realize just how much of your time, and energy, and focus you'll have to invest in this other person, just to make your marriage work, you might feel cheated. You might feel as though someone tricked you. You might feel you have been victimized by a bait-and-switch maneuver.

You might feel the same feelings Jacob felt—like you married the wrong person.

But What If . . .

But what if there was another way. Imagine with me you knew she would someday become a stranger. What if you expected he would someday be unrecognizable. But, you also had a mutual understanding that the purpose of your marriage would be growth. What if you had a common point of reference in Christ. What if the purpose of your marriage was for you, your spouse, and God to walk God's path together.

What if you both wanted your marriage to be about helping each other to let God conform each of you into the likeness of Jesus.

If you choose to approach your marriage in that way, then on that day, when you wake up next to the stranger, you'll willingly, and enthusiastically, go to work, on your marriage—even if it means working hard for another seven years.

Jacob and His Stranger

In Genesis 49, we see Jacob, at the very end of his life, giving final instructions concerning where he wanted to be buried. And he asked to be buried next to Leah, not Rachel. And he did not ask to make arrangements, to move Rachel's remains which were near Bethlehem, to the family burial site near Mamre in Canaan. (Genesis 50:25, Exodus 13:19)

For a time Jacob loved Rachel more than he loved Leah. But he persevered with Leah anyway. And maybe one of the reasons he chose to be buried with Leah is because it was Leah, not Rachel, who gave Jacob more sons in the end. And before it was over, Leah even gave birth to Judah, from whose line the Messiah would come.

Your Future Spouse

What if Jacob had left Leah? What if she never had the opportunity to bear his sons? What if there never was a line of Judah? (I don't like to think about that one.)

Jesus wants us to learn how to love people different than ourselves, and it may be he uses our spouses for that purpose more than any other person.

So in order for Jacob to enjoy and appreciate Leah, he had to remain with Leah. Instead of dumping her, he stayed with her, he supported her, he helped her to become the woman who would bear him six sons. He helped her to become the woman who would bring to the world the line of the Messiah.

If you leave, you'll never see the future version of your spouse in the way Jacob saw Leah. And there's something else.

If you *were* to leave, and you found someone new, it's just a matter of time before *that* person too would become a stranger. And the whole cycle would start over again.

The only way you're going to see your husband or wife in the same way Jacob saw Leah is to stay with him, or her.

Your Future Groom

In scripture, God calls us the bride of Christ, which of course makes him our groom. And he sees every fault, and flaw, and sin, and dark thought inside of you, and inside of me. Yet he forgives us. Even though we fall short, over and over again, he forgives us. Even the worst we have done in our lives, he forgives. He died for those faults, and flaws, and sins. Having received such forgiveness, find it in your heart to forgive your wife, or your husband. (See Matthew 18:35.)

How to Love Like Jesus

We live in an age of consumerism, and consumerism permeates everything in our Western culture, including marriage. Many today conform the marriage relationship to our culture, and define marriage in terms of economics. So many today are marrying for *me*. The economics of the relationship must be profitable, to *me*. If the marriage relationship is operating at a loss, for *me*, then it's time to walk away, we say.

But that's not how God defines a marriage relationship. For God, marriage is a covenant relationship, not a consumer relationship. In a covenant relationship, it's not about the economics of *me*, it's about my spouse. In a covenant marriage, my love manifests in serving and giving. In a covenant relationship, I love my bride as Jesus loves His bride, the church. I give myself for her even as Jesus gave himself for us. (Ephesians 5:25–27)

Your marriage, and mine, isn't a consumer relationship, it's a covenant relationship, and that makes all the difference. "The connecting link with my old self has always been the memory of the name I took on back there (when I gave my vows): 'I am he who will be there with you.' When we slough off *that* name, lose *that* identity, we can hardly find ourselves again."—Smedes

So to love like Jesus, stay faithful and stay married, even as Jesus has stayed faithful to you. You be one who keeps that name: "I am he who will be there with you." Keep that name. Even when he or she criticizes you and complains and goes negative. Even when what little good your spouse does, doesn't compare to your contributions. Even when your wife, or husband, does things that are unattractive to you.

This is how Jesus loves us, The Bride of Christ.
This is how you can love like Jesus:
Stay faithful.
Stay married.

Jesus said, "Have you not read that he who created them from the beginning made them male and female, and said, 'Therefore a man shall leave his father and his mother and hold fast to his wife, and the two shall become one flesh'? . . . What therefore God has joined together, let not man separate."
Matthew 19:4–6

Notes:
Further study will be rewarded. See Matthew 18:21–35.

1. Timothy and Kathy Keller, *The Meaning of Marriage*, Dutton Adult, 2011

CHAPTER 27

Love Like Jesus

Fast Like Jesus

*The days will come when the bridegroom is taken away
from them, and then they will fast in those days.*
LUKE 5:35

How Jesus Loved People

Jesus loved people by fasting for them.

"Wait a minute," you might be saying right now. "When did Jesus fast for people? He wasn't fasting when he said those words in Luke 5:35."

You're right, he wasn't.

But Jesus did fast for people previously. He fasted for forty days in the wilderness immediately after he was baptized by John. (Matthew 4:2, Luke 4:2) He was inspired by the Holy Spirit to fast—for you, and for me. He fasted out of love for you. He fasted to prepare himself

173

for the work he would do on your behalf. (And it's also interesting to note that every miracle of Jesus recorded in the Bible occurred after he fasted.)

How to Love Like Jesus

Jesus said, "When you fast, do not look gloomy like the hypocrites." And He said, "When you fast, anoint your head and wash your face, that your fasting may not be seen by others but by your Father who is in secret. And your Father, who sees in secret will reward you." (Matthew 6:16–18)

Jesus didn't say, "*If* you fast," Jesus said, "*When* you fast."

Jesus said of his followers, "they will fast." (Luke 5:35)

So Jesus expects me to fast—as he did. Jesus loved us by fasting to connect with God in a way that prepared him to communicate the love of God. And he expects us to do the same.

Given Jesus' expectation that we should fast, and given the remarkable results from fasting we see in the life of Jesus, I'm amazed at how few Christians actually engage in the practice of fasting.

Why do we avoid fasting?

Why will the wife on the verge of losing her husband read five self-help books, try three different counselors, and start a new exercise program, but she won't fast and pray?

Why is it the father and mother whose teenage son or daughter has begun to engage in risky behavior will cry themselves to sleep at night, they'll lament and complain, they'll pay for counseling, but they won't fast and pray?

Why is it the husband and father facing financial collapse will work two jobs, max out every credit card he has, and even borrow from his in-laws, but he won't fast and pray?

On the topic of fasting and praying Jesus said, "Your Father who sees in secret, will reward you."

So why won't you fast?

It doesn't make any sense not to.

Especially given the good news that there doesn't seem to be any minimum requirement in scripture concerning length. Jesus doesn't instruct us on how long we're to fast.

So you can skip breakfast and spend time praying for God's Holy Spirit to help you love like Jesus. Or you can skip breakfast and lunch, and then spend your lunch hour praying for the souls of people God puts on your heart. Or you can skip lunch, dinner, and tomorrow's breakfast, and pray multiple times for God to conform you into the likeness of Jesus.

You can fast to prepare your soul to love like Jesus, even as Jesus fasted to prepare himself to love.

There's no reason not to do it.

There are powerful and compelling reasons *to* do it.

Jesus who fasted on your behalf desires you to do it.

Do you really want to love like Jesus loved?

If you do, then—fast.

It will make a difference.

CHAPTER 28

Love Like Jesus

Surviving a Life of Loving Like Jesus

*When they heard these things, all in the synagogue were
filled with wrath. And they rose up and drove him out of
the town and brought him to the brow of the hill on which
their town was built, so that they could throw him down
the cliff. But passing through their midst, he went away.*

MARK 2:16–17

Surviving Power

My son Gabe drives a Tesla Model S P85D. His car has different modes he can invoke. One of those modes is called
"insane" mode. When he puts his Tesla Model S in insane mode, if
he wants to, he can go from 0 to 60 in 3.1 seconds. That's an insane
amount of power.

That power is very helpful sometimes. Like when you're merging onto the freeway, or when you're changing lanes in heavy traffic. That power can actually save you, and the people traveling with you, from crazy bad drivers.

On the other hand, if Gabe were on a windy steep downhill two-lane highway in a rainstorm, and he put his Tesla Model S in "insane" mode, and he decided to go from 0 to 60 in 3.1, he could wind up on the pavement with the local roadkill.

What you've learned so far in this book is powerful, because Jesus is powerful, and imitating Jesus by loving like Jesus is powerful. And applying that power can give you the big, abundant life that Jesus wants for us, and it can help people, and save people.

But applying Jesus' power on a windy steep downhill two-lane highway in a rainstorm might cause you to go insane. So I want to address two issues you'll encounter on your quest to love like Jesus. One is the issue of influence, and the other is the problem of becoming a Christian doormat.

Influence: Jesus and the Sinners

We see in the gospels that Jesus loved people by engaging with them, in spite of their sinful lifestyle. We see examples of this everywhere, how Jesus loved people on the margins of society. (And we also see the corresponding disapproval of the religious leadership of Jesus' day.)

There's a blog I follow called "Not Ashamed of the Gospel." The author once posted a three-part series about a ministry which reaches out to sex industry employees. I couldn't help but notice there weren't many comments offered on the last post in the series, "An Insider's Look." I think people found that post just too hot to deal with. Finally, one person commented, and, as best as I could tell, he used scripture to infer that this post about the sex industry ministry was an example of ungodly men perverting the grace of God. I couldn't help myself. I had to comment.[1]

I wrote about when the Pharisee who had invited Jesus to dinner saw the sinful woman washing Jesus' feet with her hair and her tears. The Pharisee said, "If this man were a prophet, he would know who is touching him and what kind of woman she is—that she is a sinner." (Luke 7:39)

"Of course Jesus knew," I wrote in the comment box. "But He also knew those deeply ensnared in sin need Him just as much as the rest of us."

Jesus loved people by engaging sinners.

And you should too.

What Doesn't Matter
It doesn't matter if they sin differently than you do.
It doesn't matter if you don't approve of their lifestyle.
It doesn't matter if she's promiscuous.
It doesn't matter if he doesn't provide for his family, and you think he's lazy.
It doesn't matter if she's prideful.
It doesn't matter if he's addicted to porn, or drugs, or booze.

What Does Matter
In this book, you've read about many instances when Jesus was investing in relationships with sinners. And to love like Jesus, you and I need to do the same. But before we engage others there's an important issue to address: the direction of the flow of influence. Which way that influence flows is something that matters when we invest in people.

Of course, Jesus didn't have to consider which way influence flowed, because in his case, it only flowed one way.

However, you and I are not the Christ. (See John 1:20.) I could never involve myself in a ministry to sex industry employees, because the potential is too great for the influence to flow from the people and environment I'd be involved in, over to me. I think most men rightly see it that way. All of the people involved in the front lines of the sex industry ministry featured at "Not Ashamed Of The Gospel" were women, many of whom were former sex industry employees themselves. They were ministering to other women.

You and I have to carefully and prayerfully consider this issue of direction of influence. At any time, if you sense the flow is from the people you're trying to love like Jesus, over to you, it's time to end it.

With few exceptions, men shouldn't be ministering to women, and women shouldn't be ministering to men. Someone with a gambling problem shouldn't be ministering in a casino. Someone with a drinking problem shouldn't be ministering in a bar.

That being the case, I have to ask myself, "How often have I avoided influencing someone for Jesus Christ, simply because they sinned differently than I sin?" The answer is, too many times.

The truth is, disagreeing with someone's lifestyle isn't a reason to avoid showing that person Christ's love. If you know you're on solid ground in terms of the direction of influence, love that person with your time.

Jesus did.

You must too because, *"Those who are well have no need of a physician, but those who are sick."—Jesus Christ (Mark 2:17)*

Just make sure the influence is flowing in a healthy direction.

How Not to Become a Christian Doormat

The second problem that can occur when we love like Jesus is the doormat problem. There are these two roommates Walter and Craig who live on the fifth floor of the Barnhart dormitory at the University of Oregon. Craig is on the football team. He's pretty sure he's one of the best athletes on campus. He's really into his sport and his friends, like a lot of guys are during their college years. Two of his favorite hangouts are the weight room and wherever the current party happens to be. He's a "Grand Theft Auto" and "Madden NFL" kind of guy.

But his roommate Walter is different. He's kind of bookish. He's a good student. He belongs to the college writing club. He's watched all the *Lord of the Rings* movies multiple times. He's an English major but he's taking a physics class, just for fun. He's more of a "Minecraft" and "Eve Online" kind of a guy.

Well, one day Craig has a chance to move into an apartment off campus. The day the apartment comes open is the day before a home game, and he wants to move in right away so he can have a victory party after the game. He already invited a bunch of his friends. Getting people to come to his party was no problem. But getting people to help him move wasn't working out. Not a single friend was available. So, even though he very much preferred not to, he asked Walter.

"Hey, I need you to help me move my stuff over to the apartment."

"I'd like to but I can't," Walter said. "I have a midterm and a group project presentation tomorrow." He also said yes to a request to give a presentation at his writer's club right after the midterm. And his parents were arriving for a visit after writer's club. But Walter was too embarrassed to disclose that to Craig.

"I don't really see a problem," Craig said. "I only need you for like, one hour."

Walter didn't respond but Craig could see the discomfort on his face.

"Come on Walter, don't be selfish."

For some reason every time Walter experienced a pang of guilt he thought of the dentist's needle injecting lidocaine into his gums.

Except instead of his gums, he imagined the needle penetrating his heart. And instead of pain followed by numbness, there was just pain. Craig had a knack for triggering that response in Walter. So did Walter's dad. So did his mother. So did a lot of people.

And there was that word: *selfish*. A Christian can't be selfish, can he?

"Okay," Walter said, "I'll do it."

A full four and one-half hours later, Craig let Walter go. On his way back to the dorm his phone rang. It was one of his group project partners, the only one in the group who was at all interested in helping with the project. At least until now. "Something came up," he said. "I can't do my part."

Now the whole thing was up to Walter. He thought about letting the project fail, at least in part. He could present in a way that preserved his own grade. But that thought brought out the dentist's syringe, the one filled with guilt. What would his dad think if he did that? What would his mother think? What would God think?

Have You Felt Like This?

Have you ever felt like Walter? I know I have. He's trying so hard to love like Jesus. He's esteeming others higher than himself. He's dying to himself. He's denying himself, like he's supposed to, right? He's simply following Jesus' words: "If anyone would come after me, let him deny himself and take up his cross . . ." And that's what he's doing, so he must be doing precisely what God desires for him to do—wouldn't you agree? (Philippians 2:3, John 12:24, Luke 9:23)

Well, you're right, he is right—and he's also wrong.

He's Right

Of course, Walter's right to give of himself to love like Jesus. And he's right to esteem others higher than himself. And he's right to die to himself. And he's right to deny himself. Jesus said, ". . . whoever would be great among you must be your servant, and whoever would be first among you must be slave of all." (Mark 10:42–44)

Then he said, ". . . even the Son of Man came not to be served but to serve, and to give his life as a ransom for many." (Mark 10:45)

We all know why Jesus came. He came to die and, to love like Jesus loved, so should we. As Bonhoeffer wrote in *The Cost of Discipleship*, we should die every day.[2]

He's Wrong

But here's where Walter goes wrong. And here's where I go wrong, and where you go wrong. We go wrong and we become a pushover when we leave out the Holy Spirit. Because leaving out God's Holy Spirit causes us to go from someone who loves like Jesus to someone who serves like a doormat. To see an example of someone who died to themselves and yet followed the leading of the Holy Spirit we have only to look to Jesus Christ himself.

Jesus Christ, the one who "came not to be served but to serve, and to give his life as a ransom for many," did not die, until the Holy Spirit's time for him to die came upon him. Think about it: Right after he was baptized by John, and having just received the Holy Spirit, Jesus went out into the wilderness where he fasted for forty days. There Satan came and tempted him three times. The third time they were on top of the highest part of the temple where Satan tried to persuade Jesus to throw himself down. But God didn't want Jesus to die in Satan's timing. So Jesus denied Satan's request. (Luke 4:9–12)

Not long after that Jesus was teaching in the synagogue in his hometown of Nazareth. He read from Isaiah a messianic prophecy and explained that the scripture was referring to him, to Jesus. The people who heard that didn't take it well. They were so offended, they were so outraged, they took Jesus to the edge of a cliff and attempted to throw him off. But God didn't want Jesus to die in the people's timing, so Jesus resisted. He muscled his way through the crowd, and he escaped. (Luke 4:28–30)

In his third year of public ministry, Jesus made the statement, ". . . before Abraham was, I am!" He was referring to his own divinity. And when his listeners heard this, ". . . they picked up stones to throw at him . . ." But God didn't want Jesus to die in the timing of this group of listeners. So, ". . . Jesus hid himself and went out of the temple." (John 8:56–59)

The last unsuccessful attempt at killing Christ outside of God's timing occurred one winter day when the Jews asked Jesus to tell them if he was the Messiah. At the end of his reply, Jesus said, "I and the Father are one." They were incensed at this proclamation. They picked up stones to stone him, they tried to seize him, they tried to kill him. But God didn't want Jesus to die in their timing, so Jesus "escaped from their hands." (John 10:22–39)[3]

How to Know When to Die

So, perhaps surprisingly, it's OK for you to deny someone's request, as Jesus denied Satan's request. And it's OK for you to resist and escape, as Jesus escaped. And it's OK for you to hide yourself, as Jesus hid himself, and slipped away from the temple grounds. It's OK.

You might be asking yourself right now, "But when? When is it OK? How do I know when it's OK to refuse a request, or resist a crowd, or hide? And we're also supposed to die to ourselves, so how do I know when to do that? How do I know when to die?"

It's important to recognize that not one single miracle from Jesus is found in the biblical record, until *after* he received God's Holy Spirit. Jesus Christ made every decision not to die—as well as his final decision to die for us all—*after* he received the Holy Spirit. And that's how it is for you and for me. Without following the leading of God's Holy Spirit, we'll find ourselves trampled upon. We'll find ourselves walked on. We'll find ourselves dying to self but outside of God's timing. God doesn't want that. (Luke 3:22)

You know God doesn't want that because you know that Jesus refused requests, and resisted the crowd, and hid himself, and escaped. And you know that at the pool of Siloam there were many gathered there who needed healing, but he, the Son of God, the One through Whom all things were made, the One Who is the Light of all humankind, he didn't serve them all, but only served one man with healing. And you even know Jesus didn't rescue John the Baptist when he was on death row. Jesus himself didn't serve everybody, but only served those who the Holy Spirit led him to serve. (John 9, Matthew chapters 11 and 12)

So to love like Jesus, we can't just die at every opportunity. Because if Jesus only died when led by the Holy Spirit to die, if Jesus only served when led by the Holy Spirit to serve, how much more do you and I need to die and serve only when led by the Holy Spirit to do so?

The Holy Spirit Is the Key

The key to not letting that dentist's needle inject guilt into our hearts, the key to breaking free from that guilt that can so easily plague us, the key to surviving a life of loving like Jesus is to ask for, and follow, the leading of God's Holy Spirit. It's important to know that the Holy Spirit is the key. When you look at all the different ways Jesus loved people, you might feel overwhelmed. As you've been reading this book you might have thought to yourself:

"How can I ever do all of this? How can I possibly love people like Jesus? He loved so much, and he loved in such a variety of ways. He's so amazing, and I'm so inadequate."

185

Of course, you're right. You are not the Christ, and you never will be. But as we've seen in this chapter, even the Christ was discerning about when he gave of himself and when he didn't. Even Jesus didn't help everybody.

Jesus was led by God's Holy Spirit when to give of himself and when not to. Jesus was led by God's Holy Spirit when to help, and when not to help. Jesus was led by God's Holy Spirit when to die, and when not to die.

So pray for yourself. Pray for God's Holy Spirit to lead you to give of yourself when it's time to give of yourself. And pray for God's Holy Spirit to lead you not to give of yourself when it's outside of God's timing.

Love like Jesus—according to God's Holy Spirit.

That's what Jesus did.

That's how Jesus loved people.

That's how you can love like Jesus—without becoming a Christian doormat, and without being influenced in a dark direction.

Notes:
The illustration about the dormitory roommates is a fictional account inspired by true events.
Further study will be rewarded. See Luke 11:5–13.

1. Peter Guirguis, "Club Sin: Interview With Tara Ulrich Gives You an Insider's Look at Christian Outreaches to Sex Industry Employees," NotAshamedOfTheGospel.com, 9/25/2012
2. Dietrich Bonhoeffer, *The Cost of Discipleship*, SCM Press, 2011
3. Unborn Word of the Day, "Crucifixion of Jesus was the Sixth and Final Attempt on His Life," March 11, 2008

CHAPTER 29

Love Like Jesus

Die Like Jesus

. . . nevertheless, not as I will, but as you will.
MATTHEW 26:39

It's Time to Die

In the previous chapter, we saw how important it is not to die indiscriminately. That chapter was written for people who can't say *no*. This chapter is probably more important and for a greater number because this chapter is for all of us who *don't* want to die. And at some point every one of us will have to. I'm not talking about the physical death of our bodies necessarily, but rather the time when the Holy Spirit will tell you, "Yes, it's time. It's your time to die now. It's your time to submit to My will and not your own."

You and I and every single Christ follower will encounter God in that way. Every one of us will be called upon by God to die, and frequently.

Frequently because love "does not insist on its own way." (1 Corinthians 13:5) So loving like Jesus involves dying frequently. There are all kinds of ways to do that, there are all kinds of ways to die. You might be called to die by allowing that guy at work to take the choice assignment, or by agreeing to your wife buying a new pair of shoes, or even by simply turning off the TV and engaging with the kids.

Or, it could be something much harder.

A Tale of Two Fathers

When I was growing up in Chicago, I had this friend named Danny Rodriguez. He was a great kid from a great family. And his father, Mateo Rodriguez, was one of the nicest, most likeable people in the neighborhood. Everyone loved Mateo. Tragically, Danny died in a car crash when he was still a young man. His father, the nicest and most likable person in the neighborhood, turned to alcohol for comfort. Not long after, he began beating his wife. His abusive behavior became worse and worse until she finally obtained a restraining order. One night Mateo showed up at his wife's house drunk. He began banging on the door. She called the police. He pulled out a gun. There were shots fired. And when it was over, Mateo Rodriguez lay there dead on the doorstep.

There was another man in my neighborhood, the same age as Mateo. His name is Alex Rivera. But in the beginning, he had an entirely different reputation from Mateo. Alex had a reputation for his own crazy kind of meanness. He liked to hit women, rob the homeless, and engage in other cowardly behavior. Everyone in the neighborhood was sure Alex would die young or land in prison. And like Mateo, Alex also suffered a tragic loss. But he didn't lose just one son, he lost two. The first died of cancer, the second died in a car crash. But unlike Mateo Rodriguez, Alex turned to Christ for comfort. And in the process he died to himself and he was transformed. He became a committed follower of Jesus who, to this day, loves God and loves people.

And today, everyone seems to love Alex.

How Jesus Loved People
Speaking of Jesus, Matthew 26 says,

> . . . he fell on his face and prayed, saying, "My Father, if it be possible, let this cup pass from me; nevertheless, not as I will, but as you will." (Matthew 26:39)
> . . . for the second time, he went away and prayed, "My Father, if this cannot pass unless I drink it, your will be done." (Matthew 26:42)
> So, leaving them again, he went away and prayed for the third time, saying the same words again. (Matthew 26:44)

It was time for Jesus to die. He just finished his last supper with his disciples. Judas was already on his way back accompanied by "a great crowd with swords and clubs, from the chief priests and the elders of the people." (Matthew 26:47)

So it's really looking like this is it, this is his time to die. And what does Jesus do? He goes to the garden and checks in with his Father, three times. And each time he says: your will Father, not mine. Three times he checks in. And after praying the same thing three times, out of love for his Father, and out of love for you, and out of love for me, he denies his own will and does what his Father wants him to do.

Jesus loved us to the point of death. He died on the cross for the sins of the world. But in a way, he died before he died on the cross: He died to himself, he died to his own will, when he said to his Father, three times, *Your* will Father, not mine.

Love Like Jesus

A.W. Tozer said the one who takes up his cross and follows Jesus has these attributes:

~ He's facing only one direction.

~ He's not going back.

~ He has no plan of his own.

To love like Jesus, we have to die like Jesus. Our will has to die. Our plan has to die. And we have to submit to God's way and God's will and God's plan, even as Jesus submitted to God's way and God's will and God's plan. Jesus went to God three times to confirm it was God's time for him to die. And then he died to himself. He surrendered his will. "Not as I will, but as you will," he said to the Father.

And after submitting his will, Jesus followed through and did what he said he would do: He died, physically. And he died in a way we'll never understand because he was separated from God for the first time while he hung there on the cross. And he bore the unimaginable weight of the sins of the world. (See Matthew 27:11–66, 1 Peter 2:24.)

So to love like Jesus, we must die as he died. And yes it has to happen in the Holy Spirit's timing, we may even have to pray three times to confirm it, or more than three times. But we have to die to ourselves, as Jesus died, according to God's Spirit.

The Difference Made by Dying

Both Mateo Rodriguez and Alex Rivera suffered a brutal loss, but each responded differently. What was it that caused one to go one way, and the other to go God's way? I submit that it was the way in which each of them died. When Alex lost his two sons, he decided to die to himself. He gave himself up for dead so to speak, and he submitted himself to God. Faith in God, complete humility, and absolute surrender are the keys to successfully surviving suffering.[1]

He recognized he would never understand the *why* behind the loss of his two sons. He recognized God's sovereignty. He realized God was his maker. God made his heart, soul, and mind.

Alex recognized that it makes sense that he, Alex, didn't understand the tragedy in his life.

Not understanding is exactly what we would expect concerning the God who is the Creator of all things. He is the One who created the neutron star, a teaspoon of which would weigh six billion tons. He is the One who created the flea which can accelerate twenty times faster than the space shuttle. He is the One who created the people who built the space shuttle. He is the Creator of the caterpillar that metamorphosizes into a butterfly. And He is the Creator of the Butterfly Nebula. He is the One who created atoms, and the protons, neutrons, and electrons that make up atoms. He is the One who created the quarks that make up the protons and neutrons. And He is the One who created the Hercules-Corona Borealis Great Wall, a structure made up of multiple galaxies that may be the biggest thing in the universe.[2]

Why would we think that we would understand the actions of a being like that?

That would be like a flea understanding the actions of the man who wrote the article about the flea accelerating faster than the space shuttle. It makes sense that the flea doesn't understand the actions of the author of the article describing him.

In the same way it makes sense that you and I don't understand the actions of the Author of the human being, who is also the Author of the universe the human being lives in.

Alex recognized that "these are but the outer fringe of his works." (Job 26:14 NIV) Alex recognized he will never understand all the *whys* behind the business of a Person like Him. He knew he could never understand *why*.

But he also knew his personal pain could not be because God does not love him. Because God lost *His* son too. And He suffered that loss so we can be with Him in heaven.

So Alex decided to die.

Do you see the irony here? When Alex lost his sons yet decided to surrender his will, when he died to himself in that way, that is precisely what allowed him to be reborn—as a follower of Jesus.

Then there's Mateo. Mateo lost his son but made a decision *not* to die. Mateo decided he would rather rage than to surrender his will like Alex, and like Jesus. And when he made that decision to remain in his rage, and not to die, he lost the opportunity to be reborn. And do you see the irony here as well? The irony is, in the end, Mateo's own rage consumed him, and he died anyway. But not in the way that leads to rebirth, but in the way that leads to a dark and tragic end.

Having Your Own Way

Many of you reading this book live in a privileged culture. In most cultures throughout history there was an emphasis on changing yourself to adapt to your environment. The prayers of Paul in the epistles reflect this. But in modern culture, in the industrialized nations, we emphasize changing our surroundings through technology to adapt the environment to ourselves. We're used to fulfilling our desires, pretty much on demand. Many of us live our lives with the goal of remaining undisturbed. Because if we're undisturbed, we can pursue our own entertainment.

On the surface that might seem like a good way to go, but in the end it's shallow. Soren Kierkegaard said, "The person whose life is dominated by entertainment is not master of himself at all. He is a slave to his impulses."

When we live for entertainment, when we succumb to our impulse to turn to entertainment, it's often at the expense of turning toward God. The video game or the game on TV instead of church, reading a book instead of praying to God, reading words on social networks instead of reading God's words.

And look at what God says about people who decide *not* to die to themselves. He first describes these people as those who:

> . . . *although they knew God, they did not honor him as God or give thanks to him, but they became futile in their thinking, and their foolish hearts were darkened. Claiming to be wise, they became fools . . . (Romans 1:21–22)*

And now watch what happens. In the next verse God gives them up to their desires. When He lets them turn away from Him, he does it by letting them have their own way.

> *Therefore God gave them over in the sinful desires of their hearts . . . (Romans 1:24 NIV)*

Your desires. Having it your way. Refusing to die and to allow God to have it His way, as Jesus did in the garden, it might seem good in the moment, but it leads to death. The wrong kind of death. Insisting on your way over God's way leads to a darkened heart, and ultimately to a dark and tragic end.

To Love Like Jesus, Die Like Jesus

In 1963 they found some seeds in the food stores at Masada. These were the two-thousand-year-old food stores of the Jewish zealots who killed themselves while they were under siege so they wouldn't be taken captive by the Romans. Today in Israel, inside a laboratory, scientists are growing a tree (related to the date palm) from one of those two-thousand-year-old seeds.[3]

But for two thousand years that seed from Masada remained undisturbed, and as long as it remained undisturbed, it remained a tiny seed. Then in 2005 it died and was buried, inside the lab in Israel. In 2015 it became a father. Scientists used it to pollinate a modern-day "female" date palm, so now it can reproduce.

For you and for me, fruit is born when we let go of our desire to remain undisturbed. Fruit is born when we die to our own desires and live for Jesus. Fruit is born when you surrender your life to him and let him have you, all of you.

A grain of wheat is tiny, and it remains tiny if it doesn't die. But if it does die and falls into the earth, it can produce more wheat that can produce yet more, until it's yielded a great field of wheat.

You and I are the same.

When we're all about self, when we strive to remain undisturbed, we're tiny, we're small.

Small-minded.

Small-hearted.

Small of soul.

But if we'll die, for Jesus' sake, that changes. If we die like Jesus, we can bear fruit like Jesus.

If we die like Jesus, we can love like Jesus.

So do whatever you have to do, to bring yourself to the place where you surrender your will to God. If Jesus prayed three times, then you and I might have to pray three dozen times, or three thousand times. But do you see? That doesn't matter. Even if we have to pray three thousand times, we have to do it, because what's at stake is too great.

What's at stake is our call to love like Jesus.

What's at stake is our relationship with the Creator in heaven. What's at stake are the relationships with those who see Jesus when they look at you.

What's at stake is all of eternity.

So to love like Jesus, die.

Like Jesus.

Truly, truly, I say to you, unless a grain of wheat falls into the earth and dies, it remains alone; but if it dies, it bears much fruit. Whoever loves his life loses it, and whoever hates his life in this world will keep it for eternal life.
—Jesus Christ, John 12:24–25

Notes:
1. From my notes on Joel Stephens's excellent teaching. Heard on July 8, 2018 at Foundation Bible Fellowship, Ashland, OR
2. "15 Amazing Science Facts That Will Blow Your Mind," How It Works Daily, 2016, URL: https://www.howitworksdaily.com/15-amazing-science -facts-that-will-blow-your-mind/
3. John Roach, "Methuselah Palm Grown From 2,000-Year-Old Seed Is a Father," National Geographic, March 24, 2015, URL: https://news.nationalgeographic. com/2015/03/150324-ancient-methuselah-date-palm-sprout-science/

Conclusion

CHAPTER 30

Love Like Jesus

Jesus and Your Resurrection

Awake, O sleeper, and arise from the dead,
and Christ will shine on you.
EPHESIANS 5:14

How a Man Came Down from Mount St. Helens and Was "Resurrected"

It was March of 1980. Mount St. Helens was showing signs of an imminent eruption. Greg Folsom, a firefighter in Medford, Oregon, was curious about the volcanic activity. His jeep wasn't running at the time, so he borrowed his father's car and drove to the volcano in Washington. For months before the big eruption, there were earthquakes and steam venting from the north face of the mountain. USGS scientists felt it was too dangerous for the general public and convinced the local authorities to close the area. So when

Greg arrived, a Skamania County Sheriff was there to greet him. He was denied entry into the park. But Greg knew the area. And the perimeter is so large it was impossible for law enforcement to cover it all. It wasn't long before Greg found a way in. He parked and hiked to the timberline where he spent the night. During his time on the mountain he could feel the earthquakes and hear the mountain making popping noises. But he managed to survive.

However the next day, toward the end of his hike back down, as he approached his vehicle, he saw two law enforcement officers at his car. They let him know they weren't happy with him for entering the park, but they didn't arrest him. So Greg headed back to Oregon with just one stop to make on his way. He wanted to visit his grandmother in nearby Vancouver, Washington, before continuing home.

When he arrived at his grandmother's, he was surprised to find that she was anything but welcoming. She wouldn't speak to him. She didn't even want to look at him. She was startled and frightened. Greg asked her what the problem was, but she ignored his inquiries. After about forty minutes, she finally told him that he wasn't alive, that he was a spirit. It wasn't until much later Greg learned why his grandmother thought he was a ghost. The Skamania County Sheriff had reported his vehicle the day before his return. They contacted the owner, his father, and told him Greg had died in a mudslide caused by the volcano. For about one day, Greg's family believed he was dead.

It took some time for Greg to convince his grandmother he was wasn't a ghost, but living flesh and blood. To his grandmother and the rest of his family—he was resurrected.

Jesus Resurrected

After Jesus was resurrected, his disciples were also slow to believe he was living flesh and blood. The women who saw Jesus alive at his grave told them, but they didn't believe. Then Cleopas and his friend who encountered Jesus on the road to Emmaus told the disciples he was alive. But they still wouldn't believe. Finally, Jesus himself showed up in their midst, and they were startled and frightened, and they thought they saw a ghost. (Luke 24:1–35)

But Jesus said to them, "Why are you troubled, and why do doubts arise in your hearts? See my hands and my feet, that it is I myself. Touch me, and see. For a spirit does not have flesh and bones as you see that I have." (Luke 24:36–49)

Your Resurrection

This is the beginning of the end of a book about the different ways Jesus loved people, and how you can love like Jesus. But without connection to the resurrected Christ, your attempts to follow the wisdom in this book will fail. This book was written with the death of your former life in mind. And this book was written with your resurrection in mind too. The resurrection of yourself, to a new life, even as Jesus was resurrected.

In his book *Imitating God in Christ*, Jason B. Hood writes,

> *Believers normally think of resurrection as a hope for life beyond the grave. But resurrection life is not just relevant after death. Because believers are already united to and raised with the resurrected Messiah, they are participating in a new reality that radically changes their life before death even as it will one day change their life after death.[1]*
>
> *(Ephesians 2:6, Colossians 2:12)*

The only thing is, to experience what Hood is talking about, you have to connect with your resurrected savior. I've observed that a lot of people are like the weeds that grow in and among a fruit-bearing bush. They might look like they're part of the bush. They might go to church. They might own a Bible. They might profess to be Christian. But they're not really connected with Jesus. I don't know why they do things that make them look like they're a part of the bush. Maybe they do those things because their wife wants them to, or to be with their friends, or because of cultural inertia. But it doesn't matter if they do those things. What matters is the connection. Any plant entwined with the fruit-bearing vine that isn't connected won't bear fruit. Ultimately, those plants that aren't connected will be tossed away and burned. Because you're reading this book, I'm guessing you don't fall into this category. (John 15:6)

The other group of people I've observed are Christians who are barely connected with their resurrected Savior. They're like branches partially broken off, just hanging on by the skin. They're believers but they don't have a strong connection. They're alive but not really flourishing. In my own life I've discovered what makes a difference is a strong connection to Jesus. I need to connect with Jesus in an intimate way to bear fruit. If I want to love like Jesus loved, I have to abide in the vine. I think that's how it is for all of us. (John 15:1–5)

Nothing in this book about loving like Jesus will work without a strong connection with the living resurrected Christ.

So if you find yourself in that barely connected to the resurrected Savior category, repent.

Repent is a word that simply means to change direction. So change direction. Stop trying to live life apart from Him. Stop trying to hide from your God; turn around and seek to connect with Him in the most intimate and profound way possible. Do that and fruit will flow from your life.

Do that and His love will flow from your life.

Your connection with Christ is by far the most important part you play in your effort to love like Jesus.

In Jesus name.

> *. . . apart from me you can do nothing.*
> *–Jesus Christ*
> *John 15:5*

Notes:
1. Jason B. Hood, *Imitating God in Christ: Recapturing a Biblical Pattern*, IVP Academic, 2013

Right Now Media

CHAPTER 31

Before the 7 Year Deep Dive into Jesus—and After

And he said to them, "Which of you who has a friend will go to him at midnight and say to him, 'Friend, lend me three loaves, for a friend of mine has arrived on a journey, and I have nothing to set before him'; and he will answer from within, 'Do not bother me; the door is now shut, and my children are with me in bed. I cannot get up and give you anything'? I tell you, though he will not get up and give him anything because he is his friend, yet because of his impudence he will rise and give him whatever he needs. And I tell you, ask, and it will be given to you; seek, and you will find; knock, and it will be opened to you. For everyone who asks receives, and the one who seeks finds, and to the one who knocks it will be opened. What father among you, if his son asks for a fish, will instead of a fish give him a serpent; or if he asks for an egg, will give him a scorpion? If you then, who are evil, know how to give good gifts to your children, how much more will the heavenly Father give the Holy Spirit to those who ask him!"
LUKE 11:5–13

Before I did the seven-year deep dive into studying Jesus, I wanted the people around me to become like me. But that was all wrong. After the seven-year deep dive into Jesus, I realized I need to concern myself with becoming like Jesus. And attempting to make those around me like myself is a barrier to communicating the love of Jesus.

Before I did the deep dive into Jesus, I had plans, and they were *my* plans, and I wanted God to be a part of *my* plans. After the deep dive into Jesus I want to be a part of God's plan.

And God's plan is love.

God's plan changes relationships. There have been some dramatic changes in my relationships with people I used to call "difficult" people, and with people who are different than I am. Now I don't see them as difficult or different, I see them as broken, because we're all broken. None are righteous, no not one.

And I see them that way because after the deep dive into Jesus I realize that's how God sees them. Jesus was the friend of sinners, he wasn't caught off guard or offended by the sins of others. He looked at sinners with compassion. He sees sinners as sick people in need of the great physician. And that's why God loves them (and why I didn't when I didn't see them the way God does).

Inspiration for the short passage of fiction below was drawn mainly from three sources: James Joyce's famous short story, "The Dead," Luke 11:5–13, and my wife Kathy and my personal experiences caring for someone who I viewed as a difficult person: Kathy's mother. We cared for her during the last nine months of her battle with Lewy body dementia.

There was a time when I had earned my mother-in-law's lasting enmity. And I felt the same about her. It was so bad that when Kathy's mother was first struck with Lewy body dementia, it was understood that whatever might happen, Kathy's mother coming to live with us simply wasn't an option. Our relationship was just too contentious. But then the Holy Spirit came. And what happened to everyone in my house during the last nine months of my mother-in-law's life was the greatest work of the Holy Spirit I ever witnessed. The Holy Spirit came. And He inspired us to love Mom, and to love each other: Like Jesus.

The air was too warm. The air in the house was always too warm. He gently shifted the blanket from his side to the middle and carefully drifted between the top sheet and the bed next to his wife. They were going the way of all the earth. She was going, his mother-in-law, the one in the next room who lay paling and withering. He thought of how she who lay next to him had bound herself to her mother these last few years.

Holy Spirit come.

John's eyes yielded tears. He wasn't good enough for her daughter, and for that she had hated him. She hated his hair. She hated his beard. She hated his irresponsibility and his arrogant manner. And he hated her back. He hated her platinum hair. He hated her pasty skin peppered with pockmarks. He hated her for hating him. Until He came.

Holy Spirit come.

In the other room, Esther's eyes yielded tears too. In the darkness she saw the form of a man standing in the corner. And other forms were there, children and pets and babies. Had her soul approached Sheol where the hosts of the dead reside? There was no ambiguity. To her they were there: The man threatening. The babies crying out. Her own identity was in the throes of transmutation. The material world was shriveling, diminishing.

Holy Spirit come.

Her cry of dread and panic made him turn to the door. It had begun again. He listened sleepily to the moans and cries, woeful and tortured, falling upon his ears. Time for him to rise and set out on his journey—to the other room. Yes, he was right: "If you then who are evil, know how to give good gifts to your children, how much more will the heavenly Father give the Holy Spirit to those who ask him!"

Holy Spirit come.

He was falling. He was falling upon all of his house. He was falling on every part of the plain of their souls, on the frosted fields, falling gently upon the ponds and lakes and, deeper still, gently falling into the dark rebellious parts at the core.

He was falling, upon the other room where Esther lay buried beneath the blankets.

He helped her sit on the edge and took a place next to her. He put his arm around her. She leaned on him like a snowdrift leans on a fence warm from the sun. He loved her now. He had loved her ever since He came. His soul rose above his weariness as he felt Him falling gently and heavily through his universe and gently and heavily falling, like a blanket drifting down upon one who is chilled.

About the Author

I'm Still Learning to Love Like Jesus

Some people are just naturally charismatic and have a knack for making others feel loved. I'm not one of those people. I was that person you know who started too many of his sentences with, "Actually . . ." I was that person you know who liked to correct people. In fact, I was a champion at correcting people—and if you don't believe me, just ask all my former friends. Here are some words and phrases family, friends, and co-workers used to use to describe me: harsh, stubborn, prideful, arrogant, condescending, selfish, and my wife Kathy's favorite—"Kurt, you have no social filter."

I can still be that way—I regress sometimes—I'm definitely a work in progress. To put it another way: I'm still learning to love like Jesus, just as you are. I share all this to let you know there's a good likelihood you have more raw material for God to work with than I do. In fact the value of this book is found in how Jesus is transforming me from someone who was unloving, unholy, and unlovable. The value of this book is found in how Jesus is transforming a wretch like me into someone who is—much more like Jesus than he used to be.

There's this old story, it's not scripture, or even a Christian tradition, just an old story, about Peter. And it goes like this:

Jesus was standing near the lake of Gennesaret, and he wanted to teach the crowd, but he had a problem. The crowd was too big. The people were pressing Jesus toward the water's edge. So he sees a couple of empty boats nearby and he jumps into one of them. Then he asks Peter to put the boat out a little way from shore so the sound of his voice will carry across the water and the crowd can hear him. (Up to this point everything is confirmed in scripture, Luke chapter 5 to be specific. But here's where the story becomes just a story.)

So the story goes that Jesus assigned Peter to stand in the water and hold onto the boat while Jesus taught, and the reason he asked Peter to do this is that it would keep Peter close to Jesus. *And,* Jesus knew that no one listening that day needed to hear what he had to say more than Peter.

That's how I feel about this book. Like Peter, but even more so, Jesus knows he has a problem child on his hands, so he assigned him to write this book. Because no one reading it needs to learn how Jesus loved people and how to love like Jesus more than I do. And it's the only way he can keep his problem child where he needs to be—close to Him.

I thought you should know.

I Was Blessed to Live with Some of the Greatest People on Planet Earth

I was a firefighter for thirty years. It's a unique vocation, and one reason for its uniqueness is the 24-hour shifts. During any given firehouse assignment, you live a third of your life with your crew. Most people can say they've lived with three to twelve people: their parents, siblings, spouse, children, and maybe a few roommates. Over the course of my career, I was blessed with the opportunity to live with nearly one hundred of the greatest people on the planet. Men and women who are better than me. I learned every day from those men and women. Many of the illustrations in this book are from my fellow firefighters. (For all of the illustrations, the names and sometimes details have been changed to protect the privacy of those mentioned.)

I Wrestled with this Difficult Decision

There are many authors and leaders, both Christian and secular, who are quoted and referenced in this book. Some of them are controversial. You should know that I don't agree with everything they believe. It's a decision I wrestled with and prayed about, but in the end, I decided that even though I disagree with some of what these sources believe, I still find value in their ideas. I hope you did too.

I Want to Have Coffee—with You

You're serious about following Jesus, or you wouldn't have read this far, so, let's have coffee together. Seriously, just send me an email at *kurt@kurtbennettbooks.com* and we'll set it up. No really, I mean it. I'd love to see you face-to-face and talk with you about Jesus, and learn about you. Maybe we can help each other to follow Jesus more closely and to become more like him.

And maybe we can help each other to love more like he does.

9-22

- Jeff Kotz - cancer
- Michelle " - MS

- Kevin Harding - Brain
                    Cancer

- Sam Copeland - Colon almost
                 cancer - gone

- Norma - Pancreatic
           cancer

- Joan Thomas - wife
  Jerry   " - Alzeimers
      - Hospice

- Brenda - Newta

9-29

- Bill's cousin - in PA
- Norman - hopefully son peacefully

10-6

- Praise for banquet #'s
- firm & Sophie - baptism
                 decisions

10-13

- Jen - praise -
  3 daughters baptized together
- Praise - food pants
- people in FL
- Brian - treatments

Mat. 1:18   Mary became pregnant
            thru the power of the Holy Spirit

Mat. 12:32 Anyone who speaks against the
            Holy Spirit will never be
            forgiven
            (rejecting Jesus & calling the
              Holy Spirit a liar)   Rejecting the
                                     Holy Spirit's ministry

Romans 8:26 The Holy Spirit prays
             for us w/ groanings
             that can't be expressed
             in words
             (communication beyond own
               ability to express)

Made in the USA
Monee, IL
18 September 2022